RESUMES THAT WORK

YOUR GUIDE TO WRITING A GREAT RESUME, EFFECTIVELY MARKETING YOURSELF AND GETTING YOUR NEXT JOB

TOM DUSHAJ

WingSpan Press

Published in the United States and the United Kingdom
by WingSpan Press, Livermore, CA

The WingSpan name, logo and colophon are the trademarks of WingSpan
Publishing.

ISBN 978-1-59594-614-0 (pbk.)
ISBN 978-1-59594-931-8 (ebk.)

First edition 2018

Printed in the United States of America

www.wingspanpress.com

Library of Congress Control Number: 2016916133

1 2 3 4 5 6 7 8 9 10

Acknowledgements

This book is a result of interviewing over many years, spending a lot of time reading, reviewing resumes and cover letters, learning about people's characteristics, making no assumptions, learning about methods of self-marketing for the job market, and asking the tough questions that ultimately reveal true answers about a person. I came to a realization that what I knew could help many people who were looking to better their current career position, and use the knowledge in this book to write great resumes, ace interviews, negotiate salaries, and land the job they really wanted.

I would like to thank all the people who were instrumental in giving me the inspiration, knowledge, and wisdom to realize that I could write this book, especially my father who taught me many things that have shaped my life, and have helped me be successful. One of the things that I vividly remember from him, is that on the surface, people's motivations are not exactly what they appear, and to truly have a positive impact on people, be patient and find the answers to bring out the best in people.

I am truly grateful to all who have contributed their thoughts, help, criticism, and inspiration for me to write this book.

~ Tom Dushaj

Table of Contents

About the Author

Thank you for purchasing Resumes That Work. I hope you enjoy it and find the information helpful for your career endeavors.

Tom Dushaj is a business executive with experience in a variety of management disciplines at both large and small companies.

He has a Bachelor's degree in Business Administration, Certifications, Special training in Business Management and experience in Marketing, ERP Software, Technology Staffing and Consulting, Labor Relations, Personnel Management and International Business Operations. His work experience includes personnel administration, research and development, product development, project management, management information systems, and manufacturing and quality assurance.

Mr. Dushaj has held positions ranging from a Marketing Analyst with a smaller organization, to Staffing/Consulting Manager, ERP Software Sales Manager, and product development manager roles with "Fortune 500" corporations. As a business professional, Mr. Dushaj has applied his experience and knowledge of staffing and consulting, and have helped assist his clients realize success with their projects.

Mr. Dushaj is a consulting professional who works with a number of clients in the Manufacturing, Healthcare, Automotive, Pharmaceutical, Retail, Technology, Finance, and Transportation industries.

He is active with professional organizations and volunteers his time to speak at conferences and trade shows to enlighten professionals about important aspects of their job search which includes the hiring process, effectively writing their resumes and much more.

The inspiration for this book came from the need to help people with great work skills realize their potential by taking the proper steps to writing a great resume, doing self-marketing, preparing to win in their interviews, and knowing how to close the interview by getting a job offer. It was important to write this book to make people aware that settling for the norm just isn't good enough anymore. You need to have an advantage in the job market, and be able to present yourself as the best possible candidate for the job for which you are applying.

1.) An Introduction to the Dynamics of a Career Search

I want to get hired, whom should I approach?

Bypass Human Resources and Contact the Hiring Manager: Should you contact the hiring manager, director, or VP who has final decision making authority on filling a position? Will this be frowned upon by Human Resources or the recruiting staff?

You substantially increase your chances by contacting the manager who will make the hiring decision. Yet you don't want to discount or eliminate the human resources recruiter or specialist, because there are advantages to working with these folks. Many times when you are interviewing by phone or in person with the human resources staff, you will get better insight and information on benefits, corporate culture, company policies and procedures, retirement information and other relevant information that a typical decision maker might not know.

We will talk more about approaches that seem to work better than others for contacting these decision makers later in the book. In some cases where a decision maker other than in human resources is looking for a candidate with specific skills and experience, the decision maker will make the offer directly to the candidate, and work closely with the human resources department to facilitate the hire. But keep in mind that human resources will likely check out your references, and even if a decision maker has already made an offer, it can be reneged if the references give negative feedback.

There are two types of people in this world: Those who choose their careers, and those who take what they can get from their careers. Take charge of your career by listing potential jobs you would enjoy.

Cover Letters, with or without salary requirements: Most industry experts agree that a cover letter must accompany a resume. Some job postings might even read "please include cover letter and salary requirements" or something similar to that effect. You can mail a hard copy to the prospective employer, send it as an attachment in an e-mail, or even send it in the body of an e-mail with the resume as an attachment.

You may also see a request for salary information. One reason that human resources recruiters ask for this information is to qualify or "weed out" unqualified candidates. You risk being deemed "unqualified" if your salary requirement is too high or too low. If the human resources recruiter finds you qualified for the position, you might still get called in for an interview, despite not furnishing a salary requirement. If your salary requirement is too high or low, the human resources recruiter might tell you about another open position in the company with a different salary range that might fit your background. If you are asked to provide your salary information, you have a few options to choose from for your response: you can state your salary as negotiable, state it is as a range, research what others in your position might earn, or not include it at all.

Technology and the Resume: The latest advancements for scanning and saving resumes include Microsoft Word format, PDF, Text format, ASCII and HTML. These format options have made writing and reviewing resumes easier over the last several years, especially since many potential employers accept resumes in some or all of these formats on their corporate websites. In the case of scanning resumes, we recommend a few tips to help you get through this process easily and painlessly:

- ✓ Use a clear font style that is easy to read, such as Times New Roman or Arial;
- ✓ Do not use bold, italics or underlining;
- ✓ Use double spacing if required, but check space when you are editing and see what it looks like before submitting;
- ✓ Avoid colored paper because it doesn't scan very well;
- ✓ Center your name and contact information at the top of the page;
- ✓ Proofread your resume a couple times over and always use spell-check;
- ✓ Call or e-mail the company to which you plan to send your resume, and find out what formats they accept if one or more is not stated.

Should your age be a consideration in the Employment Process? We don't think so, and many other experts don't either. Your qualifications and experience should be at the forefront as you enter into the initial stage of the job search process. Even though age might come up in an interview or during any one of the employment evaluation stages, many hiring authorities are well aware of age discrimination regulations, and they take appropriate steps to make sure candidates are treated fairly and evaluated on the merits of their qualifications.

How good is your resume? Without a good resume, you can have the best experience and go to the best schools and yet you still won't be able to get your dream job. Unless of course, you know some influential people. The rest of us must rely on a good resume to get us in the door. The person reviewing your resume will be looking for a few key items, and they have to jump out at first glance. Your resume has to make a positive first impression because hiring managers probably have 200 other resumes sitting on their desks or in their e-mail inboxes. It's critical to use job-relevant keywords, and use them in the right places and with the most effective frequency. Some examples:

"Senior Director with full responsibility for **overseeing strategic planning**, development, **training and management** of corporate purchasing and administrative groups for a $52 million metal fabricator, in addition to **leading** the organization's Information Systems, Finance, Human Resources and Safety issues."

"**Launched** a new division for a pharmaceutical company to **oversee productivity improvement and process improvement. Assigned full authority** of this group to **establish standards, policies and procedures** as well as day to day operational duties."

1. Accepted *high-visibility* public relations assignment working with the management team to launch the company's introduction into a new market.
2. *Champion* for change, reengineering and performance improvement.
3. *Positioned* organization for advanced growth for emerging markets in Asia and South America.
4. *Pioneered* the introduction of leading edge bar code scanning software.
5. *Launched* corporate-wide initiative with new strategic plans for productivity/quality improvement.
6. *Executive-level* presentation, negotiation, and closing skills.
7. *Redesigned* technology infrastructure, and *streamlined* Human Resources, Information Systems, and Finance functions.
8. Executive-level management position *leading* corporate sales & marketing and advertising organizations.
9. *Proactive* in leading the organization's strategic planning and product development initiatives.
10. Developed a *dynamic* sales culture to support sales staff and new product introductions.
11. Responsible for *spearheading* the development of a new transportation and supply-chain distribution operation.
12. Developed program to improve customer perception based on brand

and overall satisfaction of product lines through *creative* training of retail store personnel.

13. Led the engineering design group in establishing process flow procedures that helped *streamline* the number of operations it took for drawings to be approved by customer. This resulted in a savings of $655,000 over a six-month period.

14. Transitioned business from start-up through *accelerated* growth to its current position as the #1 corporation in the hazardous materials remediation industry.

15. *Drove* revenues from $4.8 million to $6.6 million within one calendar year.

16. Directed *fast-track* promotion program that increased visibility and market effectiveness for two of the organization's largest business units.

17. *Orchestrated* an infrastructure redesign of the Information Systems organization, introduced *leading-edge* technologies, and implemented security protocols that resulted in a significant decrease in spam and junk mail in the corporate e-mail system.

18. *Led* corporation through critical start-up period, and helped put it on a fast-track program.

19. Provided *vision* and strategic direction for adjustment to changes in technology and market demand.

2.) *What Employers Really Want*

Employers are impressed by candidates who have excellent communication skills, good grooming habits, and relevant work experience. Employers want trustworthy new employees who can hit the ground running, get along with co-workers and get the job done without much supervision. More qualities employers look for:

Top 10 Qualities Employers Look for:

1. Interpersonal skills
2. Motivation/takes initiative
3. Strong work ethic
4. Analytical skills
5. Teamwork skills
6. Flexibility/adaptability
7. Honesty/integrity
8. Organizational skills
9. Verbal and written communication skills
10. Basic to advanced computer skills

3.) The 80/20 Rule in Your Job Search

Eighty percent of sales originate from 20% of any given sales force. It's known as the Pareto Principle, wherein a large percentage of effects are attributable to a small number of causes, in a ratio of about 80:20. What does this mean for your job search? About 80% of your results will come from 20% of your efforts. So, to speed up your job search, you must focus on the 20% of your actions that produce 80% of your employment leads. It's really that simple.

I recommend that you sit down and add up how you've spent your job search time over the last two weeks. Did 20% of your activities produce 80% of your employment leads? If so, do more of them. Where 80% of your efforts unproductive? Stop pursuing those avenues immediately.

Here are three ways to maximize your job-searching effort....

1.) Use Your Network

According to all the research I've done and the clients and seminar attendees I've spoken to over the years as well as my own experience, up to 80% of job leads come from networking. Yet, where do most job seekers spend 80% of their time? Looking through job postings online or in the help wanted ads. But this puts you in the company of everyone else looking for a new job. Bottom line: If you're not spending 80% of your time expanding your network – talking daily to friends, colleagues, family and new contacts about the job you seek and the value you can deliver – you're not being productive in your search. Turn it around, change your priorities and make time to network every day, starting today.

2.) Make Your Resume Compelling

You have no more than 30 seconds to grab readers by the lapels and force them to keep reading your resume. If your resume doesn't grab the hiring manager's attention, you'll lose out to more compelling candidates. In the top 20% of page one, clearly tell employers what you can do for them. Back your claims with specific facts and figures that are easy for busy readers to grasp.

3.) Make the Best First Impression at Every Interview

Coincidentally, 80% of your results in the job interview come from the first couple minutes, the opening 20%. Now the good news: The first 20% of every interview is totally under your control. You make the decision on what clothes to wear, how to groom yourself, when to leave so that you arrive on time, how to smile and shake hands, what opening words to say and questions to ask.

4.) Top 9 Resume Writing Mistakes to Avoid

Here are the nine mistakes that ruin most resumes, and what you can do to prevent them:

Mistake # 1: No Objective or Summary

Start your job search off on the right foot by describing the job or field in which you want to work. Otherwise, you force the employer to read your entire resume before figuring out which position best suits you. This creates unnecessary work for your reader.

If you already know the exact type of job or title you're applying for, mention it! You can start the resume something like this:

OBJECTIVE
Engineering Manager with 10 years of design and manufacturing experience who knows how to add value to operations.

What if you don't know the job title? You can start your resume like this:

SUMMARY
Engineering Manager with 10 years of design and manufacturing experience who knows how to add value to operations.

By starting your resume with a clear objective or a focused summary, you tell the reader exactly what you want to do for him or her. This establishes a rapport and sets the stage for the resume, which will greatly improve your results.

Mistake # 2: Focusing on Your Needs

This is the biggest mistake you can make. Your resume must quickly answer the one question on every employer's mind: "What does this applicant bring to the table?"

Unfortunately, most resumes don't even come close to addressing this question, instead including statements such as, "Experienced Marketing Manager seeking a position where I can utilize my skills in an environment with potential for career advancement." While a statement like this might accurately describe your motives for applying, it makes your potential employer less interested in your resume.

Employers hate to hire new people. The only reason they need to hire someone is when they have a problem and need to solve it. Typically, they are very busy and can't spend a lot of time in the hiring process.

Writing about yourself and not including what the employer wants. Your resume should be a marketing tool addressing the needs of the potential employer reading the resume. The employer looking at this resume should be saying, "this person has exactly what I'm looking for" as they read your resume.

The success of your resume depends on making it clear to the employer how you can contribute to the efficiency of the organization. Notice this opening summary again:

SUMMARY
Engineering Manager with 10 years of design and manufacturing experience who knows how to add value to operations.

It's enticing for a manager to hear upfront that you can add value to the organization's operations. You can also say you will contribute to the efficiency of the organization or make the company more profitable, if in fact the job description calls for it and you're capable of reaching these goals. The fastest way to advance your personal goals is to help your employer achieve his or hers.

Mistake # 3: Focusing on Responsibilities Instead of Results

Stress what you've accomplished and how invaluable you are to your current employer, instead of telling the reader what responsibilities you've held at each prior job.

Make a list of your daily duties and activities at your current or previous job, and brainstorm how fulfilling those responsibilities made a positive impact on the organization. Focus specifically on results -- the more the better – because this is what the employer will want to see.

Mistake # 4: Using Too Many Big Words

I have seen this way too many times: Applicants use terminology, jargon, or fancy words that really don't have any value for the employer. The message you want to convey in your resume should be clear, concise, and to the point.

Simple is best. Use this mantra followed by national newspaper journalists: Write at a fifth-grade reading level. For example, try "organized" instead of "administered".

Mistake # 5: Spelling and Punctuation Errors

I cannot overemphasize the importance of using your word processor's spell-check. Submitting resumes with grammatical errors, spelling errors, typos or poor formatting. A potential employer will look at the resume and think that an applicant who represents himself or herself poorly on paper will not represent the organization well in person. Almost every hiring manager I talk to says they consistently see resumes with spelling or punctuation errors. In addition to using spellcheck, read through the entire resume at least twice. Focus on making sure dates, titles, and numbers are correct.

Show your resume to a few friends and have them read it out loud so you can hear what it sounds like. Tweak the parts that don't read well.

Mistake # 6: Useful Information

Hiding important information. Make your key points easy to find on your resume, and simplify or omit information of minimal interest to the employer.

Mistake # 7: Too Much Detail

Providing too many details about older jobs that don't apply to the job you're seeking. Any employer who feels your career is on the decline will consider other candidates.

Mistake # 8: Formatting

Formatting your resume in a confusing manner. A potential employer will spend about 15 seconds doing a quick scan of your resume. Using an easy-to-read format allows him or her to spend more time reading your resume in detail.

Mistake # 9: Font Use

Using too small a font, or a hard-to-read font. Resume font size should be between 10 point and 12 point.

A hard-to-read font may look something like this:

Curlz MT

French Script

Gigi

Gloucester MT

Juice

Magneto

Matura

archment

Ravie

Snap

Viner Hand.

5.) Resume and Cover Letter Myths

Myth: Your resume should be limited to only one page.

Fact: A two-page resume is fine if you need that much real estate to give employers enough information to pique their interest. The bottom line is if you need to add the extra page to tell a potential employer you can be an asset to their organization, so be it. Try not to exceed two pages unless you're writing curriculum vitae for a position in the academic field. A three- or four-page resume is longer than most employers outside academia would like to see. If you can fully describe all your relevant experience and education over the last seven to 10 years on one page, then do it.

Myth: You don't need to send a cover letter when e-mailing your resume.

Fact: Yes, you do. Sending a resume without a cover letter is like sending an unwrapped gift with the tag still on it. If you're sending your resume by e-mail the cover letter can be included as an attachment or in the body of the text. This way, if the recipient can't open the attachment, they can still read it in the body of the text.

Myth: You should list your education first in your resume, followed by your experience.

Fact: The more relevant the information, the higher up on the resume it should be. So, if you're just out of school, put education on top. If you've got a long career, put education at the bottom. The key to getting your potential employer to read your entire resume is to draw them in with the first few lines. So, if you're applying for a particular job with your experience in one industry but with a degree suited for another occupation, your relevant experience should come ahead of education.

6.) Three Creative Ways to Find a Job

1. Look Where Others Don't

As you begin your job hunt, where will you look for openings? Thinking about the classified ads or online job boards? Unfortunately, that's where EVERYONE starts their job search. Change your approach to find opportunities your competitors won't. The last place most people look for job openings is from current or past employers, contacts, and subcontractors. These people trusted you and thought highly of your skills, making them good resources for job leads. Jot down a list of at least three current or former managers with whom you are still on good terms and whom you can contact for job leads or related resources. Call or email them right away to let them know you are in the job market and explain to them what you are looking for in a job. In the course of your networking activities, you may want to let these folks know that your job search should be held in strict confidence.

2. Write a Unique Cover Letter

Most cover letters are absolutely awful. The one thing these dismal cover letters have in common: They're missing the Focus Factor. Your cover letter must focus on the needs of the prospective employer, not your needs. An example of what not to do: "I am applying for a job with potential for advancement where my skills and abilities will be utilized and where I will be challenged." Instead, try this: In place of words like "I" and "my", use the word "YOU." This will force you to shift your thinking from "I need a job" to how you can help the employer. You will notice dramatic changes in your cover letters, and you will start getting more interviews as a result.

3. Follow up Better

Most folks fail to follow up effectively after sending out their resumes and cover letters, if they follow up at all. Instead of calling employers every week and asking, "Did you get my resume?" or "Did you make a hiring decision yet?" try to add value each time you follow up. You could research the company's competition and write up a quick report, then send it to the hiring manager. Or share a success story from your past that's relevant to the employer's situation. Always ask what the next steps are in the interviewing process. Try to give employers another reason to hire you every time you contact them. Nobody else is doing this, which makes it a great opportunity for you to get noticed and hired.

7.) Tips for Applicants from Another Country

Working professionals seek career experiences and opportunities outside of their home countries for a variety of reasons:

- ✓ An opportunity for a position with more responsibility that also allows creativity, independence, and initiative.
- ✓ Getting the recognition that can be an important milestone in one's career.

Find out the corporate culture, the country culture and the culture of the person making the hiring decision. It might be a challenge to incorporate several different cultures into one document.

Some general advice:

- ✓ The terms "resume" and "CV" (curriculum vitae) generally mean the same thing, i.e., a document describing one's educational and professional experience. A CV is typically a lengthier version of a resume, complete with several attachments. The average length for a resume or CV is two pages. Don't try to shrink your font size to an unreadable level or print your resume on the front and back sides of one piece of paper.
- ✓ "Cover letters" are called "letters of interest" in some countries and "motivation letters" in others.
- ✓ In the United States, attaching photos to a resume is not advisable. Chances are, it will be tossed in the trash. There are several reasons why: Here are a just a few: 1.) If the person reading your resume recognizes your face from an incident or confrontation that resulted in a bad outcome, you can easily get discriminated against. 2.) If a hiring manager sees your photo, and you remind him of a neighbor he didn't like, or had an argument with, he might very easily toss your resume

in the trash, 3.) If a resume screener sees your photo and it reminds them of a bully or troublemaker, this might not work in your favor. Get the point. In many other countries, it is standard procedure to attach a photo or have your photo printed on your CV.

✓ Some countries require original copies of transcripts and references to be attached to your resume.

✓ Requirements for education differ from country to country. Stating your degree title is not enough in an overseas job search. You must make it clear what you studied, where, and for how many years. Don't assume the reader will know how long you studied. In some countries, a university degree can be obtained in three years and in others it takes five years to receive a degree. Also list your major and minor if applicable.

✓ Make sure you point out to the reader the details about your studies and any related projects in which you were involved. Also include training or continuous education courses.

✓ Pay especially close attention to the resume format you use. Chronological order and reverse-chronological order are popular options. Chronological order means listing your "oldest" work experience first. Reverse-chronological order means listing your current or most recent experience first. Most countries have preferences about which format is most acceptable. If you find no specific guidelines, the general preference is that a resume/CV be written in a reverse-chronological format.

✓ The level of computer technology and accessibility to the internet varies from country to country. Just because a company or individual lists an e-mail address, there are no guarantees that they will actually receive your e-mail. It's always best to send a hard copy of your resume/CV via "snail mail" just to make sure that it is received.

✓ If you plan to submit your resume in English, find out if the recipient uses British/United Kingdom English or American English. There are variations between the two versions. A reader who is unfamiliar with the other dialect may presume that your resume contains typos. Most European companies use British English while U.S. companies use American English.

✓ Don't be surprised if prospective employers in another country expect you to speak their language. Luckily, American English is widely accepted today as being the universal language of business. But you might want to draft your resume/CV in multiple languages before an interview. Some good translation Web sites include www.babelfish.com, and www.foreignword.com. But it's not enough to just translate your resume. Prospective employers will also want to hear you demonstrate fluency.

✓ It is highly recommended to have a native review your resume and make sure you use cultural terms used in the country. Non-natives tend to include terms, though correct in the exact translation, that are not used on a daily basis.

✓ Paper sizes vary by country. The U.S. standard is 8½ x 11 inches, whereas the European A-4 standard is 210 x 297 millimeters. You will also notice this size in foreign magazines, journals, or other publications. When you are sending your resume/CV via e-mail, do a "page setup" and reformat your document to the recipient's standard. Otherwise, a portion of the content will be missing when they print it. The same is true for sending a fax. If at all possible, purchase stationery that has the same dimensions as the recipient's and mail/fax your resume on that stationery.

✓ Work permits and visas are similar from country to country. Generally speaking, most employers who are looking to hire foreign professionals must be able to prove to the government that they were unable to find local talent with the required skill sets. Obtaining a work permit can take six to nine months or longer.

People around the world have an appreciation for individuals who are interested in getting to know them and learn about their culture and way of life. Be genuine about trying to fit in, and most people in foreign countries will be forgiving if you make an honest mistake. So, have fun and make the best of it.

8.) Reference Checking

Reference checking is a necessary part of the hiring process, but keep in mind that your references will be cautious about what they say for fear of being sued, sharing propriety information, or other company secrets. Expect your references to keep their answers short and to the point. Anyone who is involved in the hiring process should know the laws against discrimination based on age, gender, race, national origin, or religion. For anyone who is tasked with the responsibility of hiring the most qualified person, they will find themselves weeding out undesirable candidates by getting down to the difficult job of making the reference call. The general information gathered from references will be the basis for a decision to hire a candidate.

Reference checkers might use a generic reference release form. This form says that the employee is applying or had applied for a job with the company, and releases the former employer from any and all claims resulting from any information the employee discloses. Remember, reference checking is just one step in the process. Certain positions require an investigative background check to see if the candidate has any criminal convictions.

The unfortunate thing about references is you never know what they will say about you. Here's how you can take control of this process:

1. Make a list of prospective references. These are people who have observed your performance and can give an excellent recommendation of your skills, abilities, and experience.
2. Call them and explain you are job searching and need a good reference, someone who will praise your performance and character.
3. Tell your references the qualities that the prospective employer values, so they can relate times when you demonstrated those qualities.
4. Make sure you review what they will say about you, so you know if they will be a good reference or not. You want to prevent any of your references from telling your prospective employer anything that is untrue or saying anything that will derail your search.

Here are some basic questions that a person checking references might ask:

Tell me about the applicant's:

1.) Leadership and managerial skills
2.) Written communication
3.) Productivity
4.) Integrity
5.) Technical skills (if applicable)
6.) Short- and long-term planning
7.) Decision-making skills
8.) Interpersonal skills
9.) Overall performance

They'll also ask references about your character, why you left your last job, whether they would enthusiastically recommend you, and maybe some other closing questions.

9.) *Importance of Keywords in a Resume*

Prospective employers scan resumes to see if they have specific keywords that match the job's requirements. Using relevant keywords in a resume can greatly increase your chances of getting an interview. Remember, you are trying to market yourself; you need to use all the tools necessary to make this a successful campaign. The resume tells a potential employer that you are not only a qualified candidate, but one that would be an asset to their company.

A good way to show an employer how great an employee you are is to use active verbs that describe your strengths and abilities. Another good way to find the keywords you need to use is to look up the position where it was posted and see how it is described. Make a list of words that relate to this company's products, services and core competencies. Also find words that describe leadership skills, communication, and team player skills.

Use these words in your resume, along with "recognition", "accommodations", "awards", and "accomplishments". These are Power words. How you use these words will determine whether the reader will spend time reading your entire resume or just give it a 10-second look through and toss it aside in the not-interested pile.

Take note of common buzzwords used to describe the position. You don't have to use all of them, just enough so that the reader will immediately spot them when reading from the top of your resume down.

Note: Employers will not only be looking for keywords, but they also want proof that your experience backs up the rhetoric.

10.) Four Steps to Getting Hired

The success factors for scoring your dream job are broken down into four elements:

1. Winning resume and cover letter
2. The follow-up phone call
3. The interview
4. The thank you letter

Start by Creating a Winning Cover Letter

Hardly any job search experts focus on writing solid cover letters, focusing instead on resumes. It's true that a resume can certainly make an impact, but if the reader has to go through dozens of resumes, he or she will see a lot of similar experiences, skills and accomplishments on your competitors' resumes. So what sets you apart from the rest? A good cover letter.

Be sure your cover letter is custom-tailored to the position at hand, your accomplishments, objectives and skills, and give a strong case as to why you believe you are a great fit for this position. Do your homework on the company, and be prepared to mention how you will be able to help them achieve their goals, issues and concerns. You can get some of this information from their corporate Web site and typing industry keywords into online search engines. You might get lucky and find out some common concerns, issues, and problems in your potential employers' industry. The more research you do, the better you will be able to state these items in your cover letter. Some attention-getting items include education, accomplishments, career highlights, and company terminology that applies to the prospective company.

Following Up With a Phone Call

Call your prospective employer after you send out your resume. The phone should be just as effective a tool for you as it is for companies that use it for interviewing.

Remember to keep a record of all the positions you applied for, who you talked to, and what the next step in that process is. These notes should be reiterated in your follow-up cover letter correspondence. It will show your initiative and commitment to your job search.

Always answer your phone in a polite and courteous manner. Never answer your phone while eating, or while dogs or children are making noise in the background. Likewise, your answering machine or voicemail is a direct reflection of you. Keep your greeting short and to the point in order to project a professional image when a prospective employer calls you. A greeting with loud music or a lot of people talking at the same time is not going to score you any points with the caller. If someone else is answering your phone, instruct them to give only specific information that you want to share with the caller. They should know you are job hunting and need them to act in a professional manner.

Meeting the Interviewer

You've made it through the first two steps in the job search process. Congratulations! But don't get too excited, you still have a long way to go.

Here's a to-do list to help you ace the interview:

1. Unless you have a closet full of suits, jackets, shirts, and skirts (for women) or ties (for men), you need to go shopping. First impressions will go a long way.
2. Make sure your shoes are clean and polished. Same goes for women's shoes.
3. Your clothes must be pressed or dry cleaned if necessary. Clothes that appear wrinkled, dirty, or smelly will have a negative effect on the interviewer.
4. Make sure you are well groomed. Pay particular attention to your hair and face.
5. Do not use any perfume or cologne. You never know if the interviewer is allergic to certain scents. But deodorant is necessary.

Now that you have the grooming part down, you need a strategy for what you will say and how you will say it.

A good start is a firm handshake, then you might start off with small talk.

Example: I have heard great things about your company, I understand that ABC Company has 46% market share of widgets being made in North America.

Another Example: I read the article you wrote in healthcare weekly magazine about ways to minimize emergency room wait times and personal care to patients at your hospital. It was very enlightening.

If you plan on small talk, choose a topic suited to the prospective employer's industry to show the interviewer that you keep up with industry trends and news. All it takes is a visit to the Web to learn about the company and the interviewer. Remember, always maintain eye contact.

In your face-to-face interview, don't come off too cocky or overconfident by giving an impression that you're too good for the job or that the interviewer should feel privileged that you came in to interview with them. This sends a negative message to the interview.

During the interview, pay close attention and have your list of researched questions ready to ask at the appropriate time. Just remember that as you are being interviewed, you are also interviewing the company to make sure it will be a good fit for you.

Writing a Thank-you Letter

Once the interview is over, the next step in the process is to write a thank-you letter. Choose your words wisely. Be sure to mention a few key interests, your experience, and the value you will bring to the company. Finish the letter by thanking the interviewer for his or her time, and express interest in the company and position.

Write and send the thank-you letter as soon as you get home from the first interview.

A hand-written letter shows a personalized touch. If you don't have good handwriting, a typed letter will do. You can mail or hand-deliver your thank-you letter to the interviewer's office to his/her assistant. It is also becoming increasingly acceptable to send the letter via e-mail.

If the interviewer's hiring decision came down to you and another candidate with identical backgrounds and experience, and you were the one that sent a thank-you letter, I would bet money you would get the job.

You are your own advertising billboard, so go out there and advertise your skills and abilities.

11.) Who's Reading Your Resume?

Is your audience a human resources recruiter or manager? A group or department manager? A staffing agency headhunter? Regardless, the decision maker knows what type of person he/she is looking for before they read through piles of resumes stacked on their desk. This manager is looking for someone with specific skill sets, experience, training, and industry knowledge.

More than likely, your resume will be one of many sitting on their desk or in their e-mail inbox. Most managers are too busy to spend more than 15 to 30 seconds doing a surface scan of your resume to determine if you fall into the "spend a few minutes more on this resume" category. They will probably narrow down several qualified candidates whom they will further qualify through phone or e-mail then move on to the top three to five candidates which they will interview in a phase two (in-person) step, then with a senior manager, and ultimately will make an offer to one of these candidates.

Typically, the higher profile or important the position you are applying for, the tougher the competition will be. This manager will be looking for a person with a specific type of experience. Effective use of keywords is very important, as mentioned earlier. You risk not being considered for the position if you don't include them in your resume and cover letter.

Write What the Reader Wants to Hear

Most people are thinking about themselves when they write their resumes, not what the hiring manager wants to read. The manager is not interested in reading your autobiography. Nor is he or she looking for a friend, spouse, or interesting person. The manager is looking for someone who demonstrates that they'd be best at doing the available job.

The manager wants to hear what will make you an ideal fit at their organization, but I am not advocating that you write fiction. This resume has to be honest, but it also must focus on the part of your background that is relevant to what the manager is looking for.

If the manager reading your resume is thinking, "Big deal, there's nothing here that I need," they'll read one-third of the page and toss it. If that manager while reading it is thinking, "Wow... this person is doing exactly what I need," you've got the interview. It should not be a coincidence that the manager is finding what they're looking for. Your resume needs to tell him or her exactly what they want to hear! More specifically, give them an example of how you solved a problem or came up with an idea that resulted in cost savings or increased business, and make it relevant to their industry or line of work.

Make Your Resume Easy to Read

Too many resumes are written in the traditional paragraph format, which is not easy to read. The manager has 50 to 100 resumes and they will not take the time to read full paragraphs. They'll scan the first couple lines of each paragraph and probably will not find what they're looking for because the writer buried the best parts deep in the paragraph.

Writing your resume using a bulleted format will be easier for the Manager to scan your resume.

Whichever bulleted format you use is up to you, just don't go crazy. See a few safe examples below. Remember, bullets let the reader briefly scan your resume and see some key items that will make the reader spend more time on it.

✓

○

Give Your Resume a Turbo Boost with Substance & Depth

Making your resume easy to read doesn't mean over-simplifying your job descriptions. If you're summarizing your jobs in a few lines, the hiring manager will view the candidate as lazy and not motivated to do the job. Rather, give a dozen bullets describing your work, so the manager will think that you take on significant responsibilities and are a good employee. The bullet format enables you to say a lot and is still easy to read, as opposed to the paragraph format where you say more, but less gets read.

General Resume guideline: The standard chronological format works well if you're planning to advance your career in the same field. A skill-based "functional" resume might work better if you're making a career change, especially to a different field or to a position of higher responsibility.

Here are some examples which illustrate the above-mentioned guidelines on format choice:

Chronological resumes:
>Daniel – seeking continuous upward mobility in his chosen field.
>William – seeking upward movement in the advertising field.
>Cindy – seeking growth in a management position in the healthcare industry.

Skill-based/functional resumes:
Andrew – apply specific work skills in a new field, teaching.

General skills guideline:
There are a number of ways you can state your job objective, but carefully read the job description and make notes of the keywords, then review your resume to see where you're missing any keywords related to the position.

EDUCATION Guideline: You don't want to scare potential employers with excess credentials. In both the education and summary sections, you don't have to list all your education and credentials. If you are applying for a job for which you may be over-qualified, list only the education that's relevant.

Note # 1: If you're applying for an academic position, you might want to include your Grade Point Average and level of classes taught. Example: statistics class-105.

Note # 2: Include educational information that applies to the job. For example, if you are applying for a position that requires you to conduct training classes or seminars, it's a good idea to include relevant academic information that highlights your skills in this area.

Note # 3: A sales person's resume, for example, should include sales training classes, courses, books read on the subject, self-study, or other relevant skills acquired from these sources.

How to turn a negative into a positive on your resume:

Frank was employed as a bouncer at a gentlemen's establishment, but wanted to apply for a job as a hotel concierge. It wouldn't paint a pleasant picture if on his resume Frank stated his occupation as "Bouncer" at the Sultry Girl Strip Club. Instead, he should use "Security Specialist" employed by SGSC, Inc. Anytown, AK.

Presenting Your Work History, Education, and More

EXPERIENCE

You don't have to go into detail about the jobs you held early in your career. Instead focus on the most recent or relevant jobs, and select your most impressive job titles or the most well-known firms that employed you. Summarize a number of the earliest jobs in one line or short paragraph.

Aim to impress the reader when describing your current and past employers, by showing them that you have been with your current or past employers for a long time, showing a history of upward advancement with the company, or giving examples of projects you have successfully completed with desired results.

Put dates in italics at the end of the job. Include months, unless the job was held less than a year. Include military service, internships, and major volunteer roles.

EDUCATION

List education in reverse chronological order with degrees or licenses followed by certifications and training. Set degrees apart so they are easy to read. If you are still in college or have recently graduated, include your grade-point average only if it's over 3.2. List selected coursework if this will help convince the hiring manager that you have the qualifications for the job. Don't have your degree yet? State the expected completion dates for your degree in parentheses. Example: *B.S. expected June 2003.* Even if you haven't finished college, start with a phrase describing the field studied, school attended, and dates attended.

AWARDS & COMMENDATIONS

Include awards for "outstanding accomplishment" or "outstanding performance" under a heading such as "Awards and Commendations."

PROFESSIONAL AND COMMUNITY AFFILIATIONS

Include only those affiliations that are current, relevant and impressive. You should list affiliations like fraternities, industry non-profits, community help groups, and professional training groups, but stay away from listing political affiliations or religious groups. Include leadership roles or accomplishments within these groups if they are related to the job for which you are applying.

PUBLICATIONS

Include your published works if they relate to your desired job and field. Summarize your write-ups if you have been published several times.

PERSONAL INTERESTS

There are advantages and disadvantages to adding personal interests. Consider the following, but remember to limit the interests on your resume to those that have relevance to the job for which you are applying.

Advantages: Listing personal interests can be advantageous if they indicate a skill or area or knowledge that is related to the goal, such as pottery for someone in creative arts, or landscaping for someone in lawn maintenance. This section can tell a reader how well-rounded you are. This can also showcase good physical health.

Disadvantages: Personal interests are usually irrelevant to the job goal and purpose of the resume, and they may be meaningless if, for example, you state that you are the chair of a civic organization that has historically been known to solicit funds from the local community and use those funds for non-charity or illegal endeavors.

WHAT'S YOUR GET-HIRED "GAME PLAN?"

Start by writing your answer to this question, then prioritize the steps you'll take to get there. Now focus your writing efforts. Get a clear understanding of what the employer is looking for and what you have to offer before you begin your resume.

Brainstorm why you are the person who can fulfill the employer's needs. Write down everything you have ever done that demonstrates that you are a perfect fit for this prospective employer.

The idea is to loosen up your thinking enough so that you will be able to see some new connections between what you have done and what the employer is looking for.

When to Use Objectives and Summaries

A resume has two sections:

1.) Use the first section, the "objective", to make clear your abilities, qualities, and career achievements. Write in powerful, but honest, advertising-style language that makes the reader raise their eyebrows with anticipation and realize that you are someone special.

2.) The second section, called the "summary", is where you back up what you put into the first section with evidence that you actually did what you say you did. This is where you list and describe the jobs you have held, your responsibilities, your accomplishments and your education.

The Objective Section

Most resumes make the mistake of skipping the assertions and going straight to the evidence. The real "meat and potatoes" are in the assertions section. But don't give away too much. The best thing to do this is to leave the reader wanting more. A commonly used term in the sales profession for getting them interested without giving away way too much information is "Selling the Sizzle, not the Steak." Leave them with a bit of mystery, so they want to inquire about you to see if you are a good fit for the position.

You start by naming your intended job. This may be in a separate objective section, or it may be folded into the summary. If you are making a change to a new field, or you're young and not fully established in a career, start with a separate objective section.

Your resume should convey why you are the perfect candidate for a specific job, just as good advertising is directed toward a very specific target audience. Your resume should read as if you are absolutely clear about your career direction, even if you aren't. The first step is to establish a clear path for your future, if you haven't already. It will be easier to meet and fulfill your goals if you have a clear target. Even if you are not exactly sure what you're looking for, you cannot let your uncertainty show. A vague or broad objective will look like you don't have a positive or confident career path.

Example: Suppose the owner of a French fine-dining restaurant is looking for a gourmet cook, so he puts an ad in a local newspaper seeking an experienced cook with French fine cuisine experience. About a week later, he gets

100 resumes for this position from applicants who have experience with a variety of culinary ethnic dishes. The employer has no way of knowing whether any of them are really interested and qualified in French cuisine.

Your objective section can make your resume stand out from the crowd in the eyes of a busy potential employer. The employer is interested in hiring you for what you can do for them, not for learning as you go. So, you must keep in mind that your message has to tell the employer that you have something of value to offer that other candidates don't have, or that you can do better. Remember, you are writing advertising copy, not your life story.

Example:

"OBJECTIVE" – Talented gourmet French cook seeking a position with a well-respected fine dining establishment to prepare appetizers, main course and pastry dishes.

An on-target objective statement like this will spark their interest. In this example, this sentence conveys very important and powerful messages: "I am interested, and want the job you are offering. I am the candidate you are looking for."

Here's how to write your objective. The first thing you should do is decide on a specific job title for your objective. Ask yourself how to best demonstrate that you are the perfect candidate. Think specifically about two or three qualities, abilities, or achievements that would make a candidate stand out as truly exceptional for that specific job.

Be sure you get to the point with the objective. But remember that an objective may be broad and somewhat undefined in some cases, such as "a mid-level management position in the medical industry."

Here's an example of a more general format:

OBJECTIVE: A management/entry level/mid-level position in an organization where "x" skills and "y" skills would be appreciated (or, in an organization seeking "x" skills and "y" skills.)

If you are applying for several different positions, you should customize your objective statement for each one. You may even want to change the majority of your resume for each job you apply for. There is nothing wrong with having several different resumes, each with a different objective, each specifically crafted for a different type of position.

It is sometimes appropriate to include your objective in your summary section. Instead of this, create a separate objective section. The point of including an objective statement is to illicit a specific response from the reader. If you are making a career change or have a limited work history, you want the employer to immediately focus on where you are going, rather than where you have been. If you are looking for another job in your present field, it is more important to stress your qualities, achievements and abilities first.

A few examples of separate objective sections:

- Vice president of sales and marketing in an organization where a strong track record of expanding market share and internet savvy is needed.
- Senior staff position with a bank that offers the opportunity to use my expertise in commercial real estate lending and strategic management.
- An entry-level position in the hospitality industry where a background in advertising and public relations would be needed.
- A position in teaching mathematics where the ability to demonstrate examples and exercises are needed.

The Summary Section

The summary consists of several statements that focus the reader's attention on the most important qualities, achievements, and abilities you have to offer. Those qualities should be the most compelling demonstrations of why they should hire you instead of another candidate. It gives you a brief opportunity to convey a few of your most stellar qualities.

Gear every word in the summary to your targeted goal. First identify the qualities the employer will care about most. Then look at that list and identify why you are the perfect candidate to fill the need. Pick out the stuff that best demonstrates why they should hire you and assemble it into your summary section. Your summary should showcase abilities instead of experience. Here's an effective outline for your summary:

- A short phrase describing your profession/occupation,
- A statement of broad or specialized expertise,
- Two or three additional statements related to the following,
- Breadth or depth of skills,
- Unique mix of skills relevant to industry or occupation,
- Range of work environments in which you have experience,
- A special or well-documented accomplishment,

> ➢ A history of awards, promotions, or exceptional performance commendations, and
> ➢ One or more professional or career-related personal characteristics.

A few examples of summary sections:

> ➢ High energy, creative, and versatile real estate executive with nine years of experience in property acquisition, development, and construction, as well as in the management of large apartment complexes. Especially skilled at building effective, productive working relationships with clients and staff. Excellent management, negotiation, and public relations skills.

> ➢ Over 12 years' experience as an interior decorating consultant working in a high-profile role with retirement communities to design living spaces that cater to seniors and surrounding community events. Motivated self-starter with excellent analytical, organizational, and creative skills.

> ➢ Marketing management executive with nearly 12 years of experience in advertising, copywriting, media placement and selection, policy writing, and strategic market development. Innovative approach to creating marketing campaigns for corporate initiatives. Skilled negotiator with strong management, sales and marketing background.

> ➢ Health care professional experienced in management and program development. Expertise in emergency medical services. A talent for analyzing problems, developing procedures and finding innovative solutions. Skilled in working with different cultures, and within a foreign environment with limited resources.

The Skills and Accomplishments Section

In this final and important section of your resume, you should go into more detail about your experience. You are still writing to sell yourself to the reader. Basically, do exactly what you did in the summary section, but go into more detail.

In the summary, your focus was on the most special highlights. Now you tell the rest of the story. Let them know the results you produced, what happened as a result of your efforts, and at what skills you are especially experienced.

Remember to write as if you were advertising a product. Tell the reader what benefits they will get from buying the product: you. Don't include details unless they serve this goal.

Sometimes the skills and accomplishments section is a separate section. In a chronological resume, it becomes the first few phrases of the descriptions of the various jobs you have held. When it is a separate section, it can have several possible titles, depending on your situation:

> Summary of Skills and Accomplishments
> Recent Accomplishments
> Areas of Expertise and Experience
> Professional Career Highlights

There are a variety of ways to structure the skills and accomplishments section. Put your skills and accomplishments in order of importance for your career goals, regardless of which style you use. If you have many skills, the last skill paragraph may be titled "Additional Skills."

12.) Format and Review Your Resume

Resume Checkup & Review

Now that you've written your resume, you have a couple options regarding your next step. Your goal is to get rid of any typos or grammatical errors that might have sneaked into your resume. Some options:

1.) Have it reviewed and critiqued by a career counselor,
2.) Read it aloud…or
3.) Show it to friends or trusted colleagues.

Some things to double check to ensure the resume is consistent.

Content:

- Run a spell check on your computer before you show you resume to anyone.
- Have a friend – someone with a very good command of English and grammar – proofread your resume.
- The more people who see your resume, the more likely it is that mis-spelled words and awkward phrases will be caught.

Resume Design Tips for Resume Readability:

- Print your resume on only one side of a sheet of paper;
- Use non-decorative typefaces;
- Use a 10- to 12-point font size;
- Use 8½ x 11-inch paper;
- Use white or off-white paper;
- Choose one typeface and stick to it;
- Do not use lines, graphics or shading;
- Avoid italics, script and underlined words;
- Do not fold or staple your resume; and
- If you must mail your resume, put it in a large envelope.

Resume Format

What format fits the position you are applying for?

Several Resumes for One Job
Many job seekers who have a vast background in a variety of industries pre-pare several resumes for one job. This is done by using a chronological re-sume format. The purpose of this is to get an interview, and after you get the interview, you can bring another version of your resume to the interview that highlights your skills.

Several Resumes for Several Jobs
Write a different resume for each job you're applying for. A resume custom-ized to a specific job will give you a better chance of talking to more compa-nies than will a generic one.

Must-Have Resume Content
Most people put their past jobs on a resume, along with all the great things they did and how great a job they did. These should all be included, but with a focus on how you might perform these duties at the new company. You need to tell the reader what you can do for them, and the value you will bring to his or her company if you're hired.

Gaps in Your Work Experience?
Fill in these gaps with things you were doing. Example: Tell the reader if you were volunteering, on maternity leave, traveling, attending school as a full time student in a Masters or Ph.D. Program, or being a full-time parent. Note: It can be tricky if you were on medical leave. You will need to prove that your condition, injury or illness is past you, and that your health is either good or will not affect your ability to do the job. Be truthful, and include dates to cover these gaps.

Does Your Resume Read "Job Hopper"?
If your job history is littered with short-term stints, it's best if you combine several jobs with similar responsibilities and group them together. Some examples:

- 1985-1986 Administrative Assistant/**Receptionist**; Mortgage Firm, Highway Dental, ABC Paper Company
- 1987-1988 Cashier/**Customer Care;** Loan Bank, Byway Insurance Company, McDonalds.

If you were at an unimpressive job for a very short time and you didn't acquire any worthwhile experience or skills in that brief time, it does not have to be included. If you were employed as a contractor in a short-term assignment, and you don't have a lot of work experience, make sure to note that it was a temporary contract position. Use your judgment in determining where you got more valuable experience than you did in these short term jobs.

Matching Your Job Title With Your Job Responsibility
Replace a title like "sales associate" with a more appropriate one like "sales representative" or "account executive." Or you can use both, such as "Sales/ Account Executive". This gives more importance to the title without misleading the reader.

Tackling Age Discrimination
Age discrimination is "Unfair or unequal treatment of an employee by an employer because of the employee's age" as defined in the Webster's dictionary.

If you are in your 40's, 50's, or 60's, there is a chance that you might get discriminated against. Unfortunately, not all employers base their requirements on experience. Some may want only younger workers, and others may want only mature workers. One reason could be company culture. Discrimination happens for both younger workers as well as matured workers. Here are some things you can do to help you from being discriminated against.

You don't have to show your entire work history. For mature workers, list the best parts as "Relevant Work History" and give a description of only the last 10 or 15 years of your experience, or you should mention only your relevant job history, and state the older work without mentioning any dates.

For younger workers, you should include your internships, research work, teaching or other awards, and published works.

Leverage Student or Self-Employed Status
Employers often are willing to give new graduates or people without any real work experience a chance if they see some of the basic qualities that make a good employee. If you were self-employed, be fair to yourself and give yourself an important title. It doesn't have to be an over-the-top title like "President/ CEO"; it could be something equally important but not as loud. For example, Director of Operations, Operations Executive, or if you want to get creative, something like "Rainmaker". For example:

- ✓ ABC Catering Services (Self-employed)
- ✓ Clean Sweep Cleaning Services (Self-employed)
- ✓ Mountain View Credit Repair (Self-employed)

Make sure you have a list of references available.

What if you haven't completed your degree?
Examples of how to handle this on your resume:

- ✓ Working toward completion of an Associate's Degree
- ✓ Bachelor's Degree anticipated in November 2002
- ✓ Graduate studies in Industrial Engineering, currently in progress

Solve the No-Experience Dilemma
Go get some work experience. There are places you can go to do some volunteer work, and get some experience or training in your desired field, even if it's for a few days a week, for a month or two. This way you can put on your resume that you *do* have experience in the field for which you are applying.

One Employer for 20+ Years
You can list separately each different position you held so your advancements and job progression within the company are more obvious.

Hobbies and Interests
Many people list all their hobbies and personal interests on their resumes without considering whether it will help or hurt their chances for employment. Hobbies and personal interests should only be included if they relate to the job. If you are applying for a job as a gardener, mentioning that your interests include flower planting and landscaping will show the reader that you are passionate about gardening.

Race and Religion
There is no need to discuss race or religion with a potential employer, unless including them will support your job objective. This might apply say for example if you are applying for an administrative position at a church.

International Degrees
Phrase your academic accomplishments as they relate to the equivalents in the country in which you're seeking employment. For example: "Degree equivalent to U.S. Bachelor's Degree in Mechanical Engineering – Frankfurt, Germany"

Colored Paper
Most interviewers hate colored paper, glossy paper, or brochure-folder resumes. Use plain white or ivory paper. Never use colored paper unless you're applying for an artistic job. Besides, white paper photocopies best.

Folding and Stapling Your Resume
Folding is OK, but never staple your resume or cover letter. Use paper clips instead. It will need to be taken apart to get photocopied and passed along to other potential decision makers.

Graduate Degrees: Writing a Technical Resume

Many students in M.B.A. programs hear the same thing from employers: Resumes are too "engineering focused" and not enough emphasis is given to a business discipline. Here's how you can fix this common blunder:

- Add projects in business-related classes to the resume under the "M.B.A. Projects" category.
- Identify transferable skills from past jobs that could be applicable to a business position, such as projects that saved the company time and money or led to improved customer satisfaction.
- Include leadership positions held, teamwork activities participated in through professional organizations, community service, non-profit association member positions held, and educational classes.
- Use business industry buzzwords and terms as often as possible while keeping technical jargon to a minimum.
- Update resumes after summer internships to include business-related activities and their quantifiable results.

MORE USEFUL TIPS

Put the most important information on the first line of the paragraph to grab the readers' attention. Try not to include anything on the resume that may give the employer a reason to dismiss your resume, such as statements regarding religion, politics or race.

The job description should be a guide for writing your resume

Use a reverse-chronological order for your resume – with the most recent jobs at the top and bullet points under each job heading – if you are a student or have limited experience in a particular field, they would start with your most relevant experience at the top of the list of bullet points. Highlight specific skills in the bulleted items that meeting the job requirements.

The job description will list the important duties and responsibilities that you can use when customizing your resume to that position. It is equally important to use the job description to write you cover letter as well.

WHAT NOT TO PUT IN A RESUME

- ✓ Fluff – irrelevant information
- ✓ Salary information
- ✓ Typing "Resume" at the top of your resume

✓ Full addresses of former employers
✓ Reasons for leaving your jobs
✓ Hobbies that have no bearing or relevance to the job for which you are applying
✓ Your photograph (especially headshot)
✓ Names of current or past supervisors
✓ References

BE HONEST ABOUT YOUR WORK PERFORMANCE

If you state something in your resume, you'd better be able to back it up. A lot of employers ask potential employees to take tests to verify their skills. Employers also role play in the interview process, in addition to an extensive Q&A about background and experience to see how well you know your job, how well you did it, and how you can apply your skills and experience to help this employer solve their problems. You should communicate honestly what you did best and explain in detail how you rose above and did an excellent job at previous employers.

Proofread Your Resume

ProofdReading is imfortant – (see what I mean)

It's critical to proofread your resume. Look it over at least twice and use a spell checker. Lastly, let someone critique and proofread it who proofreads documents as part of their job duties. Friends who teach, write, or work in human resources make good proofreaders. Don't give potential employers an excuse to dismiss your resume because of typos, grammatical errors, and misspellings.

Types of Resumes

The Four Basic Resume Formats

There are four basic types of resumes: Chronological, Functional, Combined (Chronological/Functional), and Targeted. See examples of all four below, but note that these are typical examples and should only be used as a guide to see how the formats differ from each other.

Chronological

The chronological resume structure is the most traditional resume format. The experience section becomes the focal point of the resume because each of your past jobs is described in detail, along with sections of skills and/or accomplishments at the beginning of the resume. This format is primarily used when you are staying in the same profession, in the same type of work. The chronological resume should always have an objective statement or summary section to grab the reader's attention.

Advantages: Traditional, conservative readers like this format best because it's easy to understand your current and former job duties. This format highlights the employer, especially if this past position was impressive.

Disadvantage: This format is rarely appropriate for someone making a career change. It's also more difficult to highlight what you do best in the chronological format.

Functional
The functional resume is a highlight of your major skills and accomplishments from the beginning. This helps the reader to clearly see what you can do for them, instead of having to read through the job descriptions to find out. This format is best if you are planning on going into a new career direction or field because it focuses on key skills and qualifications you have from past employers. This shows a prospective employer that you are a successful applicant in your field. While the functional resume is a must for career changers, it is also appropriate for those with divergent careers, those with a wide range of skills in their profession, military officers, students, and for homemakers returning to the job market.

Advantages: It is a very effective type of resume, and is highly recommended. It can help you reach a new goal or direction.

Disadvantages: The functional format makes it hard for the employer to know exactly what you did in each of your jobs, which could be a problem for some interviewers.

Combined

A combined resume has elements of both a chronological and functional format. It's typically a shorter chronology of job descriptions followed by a brief skills and accomplishments or qualifications section. It may also be a standard functional resume with your accomplishments for the different jobs held.

Advantages: The combined format shows advantages of both kinds of resumes, avoiding the potential negative effects of either type.

Disadvantage: The combined format makes for a longer resume. It can also be repetitious: You can highlight your accomplishments and skills in both the "functional" section and the "chronological" job descriptions.

Targeted Resume

This is a customized format that specifically highlights the experience and skills you have that are relevant to the job you are applying for. When you are writing a targeted resume, you need to know what audience is going to read your resume. The key here is to match up your real skills and experience to the position for which you are applying.

Sample Resume Formats

<u>**Sample Chronological Resume – Retail Sales**</u>

James Hudson
234 Union Street
New York, New York 10010
(Home) 212-234-8888 (Mobile) 212-808-8888
Jimh0011@yahoo.com

Experience

Merchandise Specialist, Macy's
January 2010 – Present

- Greeted customers upon entering the store and assisted with purchase of products.
- Restocked merchandise and handled shipment of products.
- Handled placement of merchandising banners, signs, and displays throughout the store.
- Responsible for cashing out register at the end of first shift.
- Performed monthly inventory counts and re-orders for several departments throughout store.
- Coordinated invitations to send to preferred customers for VIP in-store sales promotional events.

Sales Associate, Neiman Marcus
June 2007 – January 2010

- Responsible for opening store and stocking and arranging merchandise for children's department.
- Assisted in unloading inventory and setting up seasonal fashion clinics for the store.
- Attended fashion seminars and assisted with training and mentoring of new sales associates.
- Worked closely with in-house tailors and seamstresses for customer fittings.

Cashier, Best Buy
July 2005 – June 2007

- Performed cashier duties, such as scanning products, accepting currency from customers, providing receipts for all purchases, telling customers about some of the benefits and savings when signing up for the Best Buy charge card, and cashing out at the end of shift.

Education

Daytona Beach Community College, Daytona Beach, Florida 1985 to 1987

Computer Skills

- Proficient with all Microsoft Office applications, including Word, Excel, Access and PowerPoint.
- Computer Platforms – PC, MAC – IE, Chrome, Firefox, and Opera.
- Operating Systems – Microsoft Windows 2000, XP, and Apple Macintosh OS.

Sample Functional Resume – Sales Management Position

Adam J. Johnson
3258 Carlyle Place
Boston, MA 12345
888-221-1000
email: jimbo876@cable1.com

OBJECTIVE

To secure a position in the automotive parts industry where I can showcase my sales leadership skills, sales training, and superior customer service skills. I can confidently set achievable sales goals and bring value to the organization with my knowledge of the automotive parts industry and successful track record of motivating sales professionals.

SUMMARY OF QUALIFICATIONS

High-energy managerial professional with a successful record of achievement in the automotive industry. Extensive knowledge in plastic materials, manufacturing and injection molding processes. Highly motivated, results-driven team player. Conducted sales training seminars for several Fortune 500 companies since 1998. A sales management professional with attention to detail, strong business acumen and a very good customer service satisfaction rating. Fully understand Union work environments and how to successfully co-exist in this environment. Other major strengths include strong leadership skills, excellent communication skills, hiring, termination, event scheduling, and other administrative tasks. Computer literate with extensive knowledge of compliant manufacturing processes.

PROFESSIONAL ACCOMPLISHMENTS

National Sales Manager
Developed successful training programs for the sales staff and increased sales by 24% for the year 2016. Assigned smaller accounts to junior sales representatives and mentored their progress and activities.

Responsible for daily sales operations, including but not limited to performance reviews, accountability and quota tracking for all sales staff. Also responsible for delegating responsibility to senior sales representatives when appropriate.

In addition to supervising a sales team of 12 people, I was directly involved in conflict resolution, training in telephony and customer care, resource scheduling, and special projects.

Reduced sales staff employee turnovers, introduced Wi-Fi laptops and tablets to enable sales staff to effectively communicate with headquarters to track customer orders and inquiries via the internet.

EDUCATION

Master of Business Administration – Harvard University – 1982 to 1984
Bachelor of Science in Marketing – University of Southern California, Los Angeles, CA – 1978 to 1982
Associate of Arts in Business Administration – San Diego University, San Diego, CA – 1976 to 1978
Sandler Sales Method Training – 1996
Dale Carnegie Courses in Motivating Sales Teams – 1990

References available upon request

Sample Combination Resume – Sales Management Position

Adam J. Johnson
3258 Carlyle Place
Boston, MA 12345
888-221-1000
email: ajj901@cable1.com

OBJECTIVE

To secure a position in the automotive parts industry where I can showcase my sales leadership skills, sales training and superior customer service skills. With my knowledge of the automotive parts industry and successful track record of motivating sales professionals, I can confidently set achievable sales goals and bring value to the organization.

SUMMARY OF QUALIFICATIONS

High-energy managerial professional with a successful record of achievement in the automotive industry. Extensive knowledge in plastic materials, manufacturing and injection molding processes. Highly motivated, results-driven team player. Conducted sales training seminars for several Fortune 500 companies since 1998. A sales management professional with attention to detail, strong business acumen and a very good customer service satisfaction rating. Fully understand Union work environments and how to successfully co-exist in this environment. Other major strengths include strong leadership skills, excellent communication skills, hiring, termination, event scheduling and other administrative tasks. Computer literate with extensive knowledge of compliant manufacturing processes.

PROFESSIONAL ACCOMPLISHMENTS

National Sales Manager
Developed successful training programs for the sales staff and increased sales by 24% for the year 2016. Assigned smaller accounts to junior sales representatives and mentored their progress and activities.

Responsible for daily sales operations, including but not limited to performance reviews, accountability and quota tracking for all sales staff. Also responsible for delegating responsibility to senior sales representatives when appropriate.

In addition to supervising a sales team of 12 people, I was directly involved in conflict resolution, training in telephony and customer care, resource scheduling, and special projects.

Reduced sales staff employee turnovers, introduced Wi-Fi laptops and tablets to enable sales staff to effectively communicate with headquarters to track customer orders and inquiries via the internet.

WORK HISTORY

Automotive Plastics Supplier – National Sales Manager, Chicago, IL 1999 - 2006
Hewlett Packard – Sr. Sales Representative, San Diego, CA 1995 - 1999
Arthur Manufacturing – Sales Representative, Fresno, CA 1990 - 1995
Wal-Mart – Warehouse Supervisor, Milpitas, CA 1988 - 1990
Paramount Art Gallery – Shipping Supervisor, Sacramento, CA 1986 – 1988

EDUCATION

Master of Business Administration – Harvard University - 1984 to 1986
Bachelor of Science in Marketing – University of Southern California, Los Angeles, CA. - 1980 to 1984
Associate of Arts in Business Administration – San Diego University, San Diego, CA. - 1978 to 1980
Sandler Sales Method Training – 1996
Dale Carnegie Courses in Motivating Sales Teams – 1990

References available upon request

Sample Targeted Resume - Human Resources

Adam J. Johnson
3258 Carlyle Place
Boston, MA. 12345
888-221-1000
email: jimbo@cable1.com

SUMMARY OF PROFESSIONAL QUALIFICATIONS

Experienced manager with expertise in human relations and project management

Extensive background in staff recruitment and retention

Staff training and development

Superb written and oral communication skills

Organizational and strategic planning

Management coaching

Program marketing

Contract negotiation and compliance

Knowledge of federal and state employment law

PROFESSIONAL AFFILIATIONS

American Management Association

American Marketing Association

Toastmasters International

PROFESSIONAL EXPERIENCE

National Sales Manager
Automotive Plastic Supplier – 2009 to 2016

Developed successful training programs for the sales staff and increased sales by 24% for the year 2016. Assigned smaller accounts to junior sales representatives and mentored their progress and activities.

Responsible for daily sales operations, including, but not limited to, performance reviews, accountability, and quota tracking for all sales staff. Also responsible for delegating responsibility to senior sales representatives when appropriate.

In addition to supervising a sales team of 12 people, I was directly involved in conflict resolution, training in telephony and customer care, resource scheduling, and special projects.

Reduced sales staff employee turnovers, introduced Wi-Fi laptops and tablets to enable sales staff so they could effectively communicate with headquarters to track customer orders and inquiries via the internet.

Sr. Sales Representative
Hewlett Packard – 2008 to 2016

Developed successful training programs for the sales staff, and increased sales by 24% for the year 2002. Assigned smaller accounts to junior sales representatives and mentored their progress and activities with those assigned customers.

Responsible for daily sales operations, including but not limited to performance reviews, accountability and quota tracking for all sales staff, and assigning/delegating responsibility to senior sales representatives when appropriate.

In addition to supervising a sales team of 12 people, I was directly involved in conflict resolution, training in telephony and customer care, resource scheduling, and special projects.

Reduced sales staff employee turnovers, introduced Wi-Fi laptops and tablets/phones to enable sales staff to effectively communicate with headquarters to track customer orders and inquiries via the internet.

Sales Representative
Arthur Manufacturing, Inc. – 2006 to 2008

Directly responsible for cold calling, which included qualifying leads, meeting with customers, understanding their needs, showing product demonstrations, preparing proposals, and closing the sale. Was honored the Sales Champion Award for three straight years for surpassing quota by 30%. Assigned smaller accounts to junior sales representatives and mentored their progress and activities with those assigned customers.

Improved customer service for my customers, including Office Depot, General Electric, and Merck Pharmaceuticals. I earned all these sales through relationship building and excellent account management.

I was directly involved in conflict resolution with customers, customer care, and handling special projects that required creative financing to acquire customers' business.

EDUCATION

Master of Business Administration – Harvard University – 1984 to 1986

Bachelor of Science in Marketing – University of Southern California, Los Angeles, CA – 1980 to 1984

Associate of Arts in Business Administration – San Diego University, San Diego, CA – 1978 to 1980

Sandler Sales Method Training – 1996

Dale Carnegie Courses in Motivating Sales Teams – 1990

13.) Resumes and the Internet

Electronic resumes typically use these formats:

- Microsoft Word Format
- ASCII & Text Format
- HTML Web Resumes

We will to cover these formats more in detail, so you can decide which format best suits your resume.

Microsoft Word Format

A Microsoft Word-formatted resume is the most commonly used format right now, and the Word versions used range from Windows Office to 2010, 2011, 2013, 2016, and Office 365. The Word version is widely used because it allows you the ability to change font sizes and types, add clip art and add borders. This version is easy to send as an attachment via e-mail.

ASCII & Text Format

ASCII-formatted resumes have some limitations when it comes to the creativity of your resume because this format is primarily a text type format. You will find that the formatting enhancements, like bold, italics and lines have been stripped from the resume. Most application formats that are ASCII-based will automatically replace bullets with asterisks (*). It's a good idea to spell out percentage signs (& and %), because some scanners have difficulty interpreting these symbols.

HTML Web Resumes

In the past few years, HTML or Web resumes have played an increasingly important role in online job searching, especially for those seeking employment in high-tech and creative fields. HTML formats have benefits for those who need a broader portfolio of formatting. Web pages have some benefits that can be an advantage when it comes to being creative with your resume. You can include photo images, hyperlinks to other web sites, graphics and streaming video just to name a few options. Whether you consider an online version or a one-page HTML resume, these Web-based documents give your resume an attractive appearance and flexibility with a few options. But beware that you'll probably want to clean up any extra spaces or gaps caused by tabs.

Tips for Sending Resumes Via E-mail

Beware of spam filters! Your resume can get caught up in a spam filter and never received by the potential employer. It is becoming increasingly more difficult to get e-mails through corporate spam filters as companies tighten their security and spam rules. Spam filters will normally scan the e-mails for particular words that are common to spam type e-mails, so be smart and use Power words (see chapter 16 on Power words) in the body of the text and the subject line of your e-mail.

Many employers now advise potential candidates to send resumes as e-mail attachments, rather than mailing them through the postal service. This saves the employer time and allows them to make a quicker hiring decision.

Consider applying online through a job posting ad. It's a safe way to know that your resume will get to the intended recipient. But don't forget to note the contact person's name, e-mail address, company name and address if provided.

Important: Make sure you send the resume as the advertisement instructs. Be sure to note a reference number from the advertisement and address it to the correct person.

Should you prepare different versions of your resume?

Many recruiting experts recommend you do keep duplicates of your resume in each of these versions or formats. Keep in mind that this is the same document presented in four formats. Each can be requested from potential employers for a specific delivery purpose.

1. **Plain Text Version**: A plain text file is ready to copy and paste into online forms or to post in online career website databases. This is called an ASCII copy.
2. **Print Version (a.k.a. Hard Copy)**: This version could have bullet points, italics, bold text, and other highlights. It will be ready to either mail out to potential employers or hand to potential contacts for interviews. This can be created in Microsoft Word and other formats.
3. **Scanned Version**: A more limited designed version without all the fancy design highlights helps to keep it simple.

4. **HTML Web Version**: This version offers a variety of font formats, graphics, borders and animation.
5. **E-Mail Format (in body of text):** There are some limitations to what you can add here. In some e-mail applications, you might be restricted to just plain text without any options to change fonts or sizes. This would be considered an ASCII plain text format. In other e-mail applications, such as HTML, you can change font sizes and color, and add images or graphics in JPEG or GIF formats.
6. **Portable Document Format (PDF):** The benefits of this version include the content being locked exactly as you entered it and the file size, which is significantly smaller than a scan, especially if scanned in color. Most word processing programs will enable you to "print to" PDF if desired.

Web-Based Formats

HTML Version

There are many reasons why job seekers prefer an HTML version for their resumes. Job seekers in the creative arts field especially seem to prefer it to other versions. But if done right, this version can be used in a variety of fields.

- Start with a basic HTML version of your resume. Try to avoid huge graphics or other additions that will make your file take a long time to load. You want your resume to be viewed quickly by the reader.
- Consider your resume as a portfolio; it should have links to past employers and projects you have worked on available via the internet.
- Make sure you put only relevant information that the potential employer will find interesting and valuable.
- Keep your image for your portfolio professional; this is how you want to be known.

Plain Text on Career-builder Websites

- Most career-builder websites force you to use a pre-set resume format. Most online form-builders insist on a chronological resume format, which focuses on work history. Career changers are better off using a functional resume.
- Career-builder websites don't let you save your work and reuse it. You will probably have to repeat your effort for every database you encounter. Fortunately, there are career websites that partner with a few of the bigger ones, and this means postings on one site propagates to others. When you post your resume on these career websites, it's best to check where else your resume will appear. You might not want it to be on all the affiliated websites.

- Career-builder websites don't let you spell check as you can with Microsoft Word. With an HTML format, your formatting options are limited.

Tips for writing your resume in web formats

✓ Do not use lines or borders
✓ Do not use bold print, italics, or underlining
✓ Leave large margins all the way around the resume
✓ Avoid using colored paper, stick to white or a very light ivory
✓ Be sure to center your name, address and phone number in the header of the page
✓ Check keywords to make sure you have included them to define your job duties and qualifications
✓ Use CAPS for important or special emphasis words

Rules for Responding Online

There are some simple rules to follow if you want to play in this cyberspace. You have about 15 seconds to grab your reader's attention, so make your message unmistakably clear. Your mission is to convince the potential employer to:

- Open your e-mail
- Spend some time reading your message
- Not delete your e-mail
- Respond to your e-mail

You want to do your due diligence here, because it is important that every aspect of this e-mail campaign is correct.

Here is a guideline of what needs to be covered:

Don't make the reader's job harder. You'll give them an excuse to trash your resume if you use the wrong format, forget to include an advertisement ID number, misspell contact person's name, or fail to read the instructions on how to submit your resume. Getting your e-mail opened, read and actually considered comes down to some simple rules.

1. Type the recipient's e-mail address correctly. You don't want your resume to be sent to the wrong person and deleted without being read.
2. Send your resume in the body of the e-mail, not as an attachment.
3. Read instructions from career websites carefully, in case you need to include things like reference numbers.
4. Include a cover letter in the e-mail. You can include a couple paragraphs in the body of the e-mail or send it as an attachment.

5. Use the correct subject in the subject line. Too many people put their name, the date and the word "resume". This spells automatic deletion. Remember, you are applying for this job along with many other people. Make your subject line better than everyone else's. Example: "Financial Wizard seeking dynamic organization." You can be creative here, but be truthful too.
6. Research the prospective company's website. Learn what they do and also use some industry keywords from the website in your resume.
7. Include all your contact information in the resume and the body of the e-mail text. Make sure your contact information is clearly displayed in a larger font style along with your phone number.

14.) *Social Media for the Job Search*

Social media in its many forms have become an important element in our daily lives, both in business and private life. We have an insatiable need to be connected with each other at different levels. Fortunately for many of us, there are multiple venues where we can do this. The job search component is an important part of that connectivity.

Companies of all sizes have been using social media as a way to further screen applicants for their company positions for some time now. It's sort of a new version of the background check method. Potential employers verify dates, employers, titles, roles, and other public information that they can find to verify information they have gathered about you.

What is Social Media?

Social media is a collection of websites and application enablement tools that empower the public to participate in social networking to let their voice be heard. With the introduction of new technologies, platforms and websites that cater to social media, it's becoming easier to communicate with recruiters, hiring managers, friends, family and various business contacts that may have job opportunities, or know of people who are hiring. There's the inherent human connectivity factor that allows us to express our opinions, thoughts, and ideas that some organizations might be attracted to and might consider valuable.

Why is Social Media so important to your job search?

Social media is one of the most important forms of communication available to the masses. It offers a vast array of platforms to communicate your message to let people know that you are the candidate they should hire. Recruiters and business professionals have been using social media for years, and rely on it to source candidates for their job openings.

Here are some top social networking sites for job searches

1.) Facebook
2.) Twitter
3.) LinkedIn
4.) Pinterest
5.) Google+

Let's look at some social media platforms.

LinkedIn

Largely used by business professionals. LinkedIn is a large professional network where you can connect with other business professionals. You can create or participate in discussion groups, or interact at a social level. LinkedIn has over 450 million members (2016) and is widely viewed as a business/professional social networking site. Co-workers, friends, and clients are able to endorse the skills you list in your profile, and anyone who's worked with you at your listed jobs is able to leave you a review about the work you did for them.

LinkedIn is being used more and more by employers to find qualified job applicants, and screen for potential contacts that could add value as a connection, and possibly a referral for a job applicant. Here's how to get started.

- If you don't have a LinkedIn account, you can go to linkedin.com to register and create a profile. Complete the basic and additional information sections of your profile.
- Update your work history, experience, education, accomplishments, certifications, or other relevant skills you have acquired that will showcase your skill set. Keep it professional.
- Start using job search tools on LinkedIn to generate interest from companies and recruiters.
- Include a professionally dressed headshot photo.
- Connect with business associates that you know, alumni, and new ones that you meet on a regular basis.
- Post your best work. (If there's no copyright restrictions).
- Join groups in your industry, be active, follow organizations that interest you, and participate in discussions from thought leaders. The more connections you have, the better your chances of exposure to new opportunities.

Twitter

A free microblogging service which allows registered members to stay connected via short posts with friends, family, co-workers, organizations, industries, and professionals. This form of communication is called "tweeting", and can include links, photos, and video. These short posts are limited to 140 text characters. Here's how to get started.

- Create a Twitter handle and professional profile.
- Build a respectable profile with your opportunity interests and any links to your website (if you have one), or social media accounts.
- Establish connections with friends, co-workers, and high value people.
- Share your content and expertise, opinions, industry knowledge, and samples of your work.
- Upload a professional headshot photo.
- Build credibility by answering questions or voting on polls of interest.
- Look up articles and tweets of interest, follow, reply, and retweet.
- Do a job search by title, location, company, or specific contact.
- Follow hashtags. Here's what they would look like: #Sample.

Facebook

Chances are, you probably use Facebook to connect to friends and family. Facebook has expanded its reach into professional networking, given it already has many of the professional contacts you would find in other social media platforms. This is just another way to extend your reach out to professionals that could be of value to your network. When creating a Facebook account, you may want to keep your personal and professional profiles separate.

- Look for positions that you can apply for through Facebook. This is typically done through links that take you to external career websites with job postings.
- Most Social Media platforms have like buttons so you can like an article, photo, or posting. A good way to start is to "like" your own Facebook profile, and other social media sites where you are a member.
- Post a video that shows your professional presentation, speaking, and problem solving skills.
- Be real to your audience. Showing you are genuine and authentic shows character.
- Start discussions, answer questions, offer links with informative content, and comment on posts where you can add value, and at the same time build credibility.
- Customize your profile settings so you can have control over who sees personal content and professional content. This can be accomplished using the friend list feature in your privacy settings.

Google+

Google+ (pronounced Google Plus) is an interest-based social network platform owned by Google. You can import your contacts, assign them to circles of interest, and connect with communities of other Google users. You can also log into your Google account, do location check-ins, and instant uploads from your camera. Google+ also offers Circles (personalized social circles), and Hangouts (video chat and instant messaging). Here's how to get started.

- Circles and Hangouts…create an account for circles and hangouts, and include a resume/CV profile, and invite recruiters, friends, industry professionals and people of interest.
- Participate in conversations with interest groups, share content (articles, photos, and videos).
- Let your groups know what type of position or opportunity you are seeking.

Pinterest

This platform is content rich in the creative marketing, graphic arts and visual display arena. It provides a creative way to showcase your talents and exhibit your creative side. Postings on Pinterest are called "pinning". These can be displayed as a collection of pins with a common theme.

- ✓ Come up with a creative headline that highlights your top five accomplishments.
- ✓ Draft an infographic resume that includes images or illustrations of your work, and visual graphics that help illustrate messaging. If you have a difficult time designing graphics for the graphic version of your resume, there are applications that can help you with that like Kinzaa, Re.vu, Easelly, Visual CV, and CeeVee, just to name a few.
- ✓ Add links to your profile like photos, videos, and professional information.

8 Social Media Career-Ending Mistakes to Avoid

Social media if used properly could mean the difference between getting the job you want, or making a mistake that could prevent you from getting the job you have applied for. Here are a number of social media mistakes that you should steer clear of. We are more electronically connected than ever before, and with connections comes the responsibility to be wise about what you post, where you post, and how you are viewed on social media platforms. Here are some examples.

1.) Be careful what you say

It's easy to get caught up in a discussion or post about an incident that happened where you might vent or post a derogatory opinion about a race, religion, nationality or group that might be sensitive to a lot of people. Whether you meant to post it as a joke or a prank, a lot of people might see it, including your employer or prospective employer, and they might have a negative opinion about your post or opinion, and they might take it the wrong way, which could mean your job.

2.) Watch what and where you post

Be mindful of what you post, and where you post it. Posting an inappropriate photo of yourself in a compromising situation, for example, will land you in hot water if someone you work with, or someone you interviewed with sees it. Also, stay away from posting photos of yourself while intoxicated. These types of behavior might not be what the company wants in their candidates. Also, don't assume a potential employer is only checking one of your social media profiles. They check LinkedIn, Facebook, Twitter, Google, Instagram, and other public profiles they may find online about you.

3.) Badmouthing your company or boss

Negative venting about your job, company or boss is never a good idea. Remember the world-wide-web is open 24/7, and you never know if a colleague knows the person you may be badmouthing. Negative talk almost always gets back to people in no time. You don't want it to come back and haunt you if you're about to get a job offer or promotion. This badmouthing might also affect future job opportunities, too.

4.) Poor use of spelling, punctuation, and grammar in your posts

This will give the reader an indication that you lack the ability to clearly communicate your message and ideas effectively. You don't want to get written off before you have a chance to prove your worth to a company because of typos or poorly written posts or comments.

5.) Posting personal information about job offers, interviews, income, etc.

Personal information is simply that. Personal. Confidentiality is critically important when it comes to your livelihood and how you earn a living. With increased risks of personal accounts getting hacked, and personal information stolen, we should be even more protective of our personal information. If you post that you received a job offer, and criticize the offeror because it wasn't exactly what you wanted or they tried to low-ball you, don't resort to any disrespecting comments. It's just not a good idea.

6.) Plagiarizing

I can't stress enough the importance of using your own content, material, and voice. Plagiarism is most definitely frowned upon in any shape or form. It has no place in the business world. It is wrong at many different levels, and speaks volumes about the lack of creativity, integrity, and business ethics. If you're quoting an article, posting a photo or tweet, give credit where credit is due, and cite the source and author.

7.) Badmouthing your customers

We all have days where things don't go as smoothly as we would like. Maybe your customer is giving you a hard time about an order or complaining about your product or service. Whether you work in the corporate world, retail, or a service industry, it's never a good idea to badmouth your customers, especially if you post it on social media. It shows your company or business in a negative light. Don't make these mistakes, because they could be detrimental to your career or job.

8.) Zero presence on Social Media

Not having a presence on any social media platforms could hurt your chances if a potential employer is looking to find information on your character, background, history, education, charity work, or general information that may help them to see if or what kind of profile you may have. If they don't find anything on you, they may get suspicious, and decide not to pursue you as a potential employee.

5 additional tips to ensure that Social Media will help you land your next job.

The social media component has become an important part of the job search process strategy, but it shouldn't completely replace your job search. Establishing a professional presence and becoming a valued resource to potential employers is a good start.

1.) Engage and stay active online.

Participating and being active online shows that you are serious about contributing to meaningful conversations. Following links is a good way of staying on top of industry news and topics of interest. Establish yourself as an industry expert by commenting on questions with relevant answers and following links and posts. After spending some time on several social media platforms, you'll get an idea of which ones are used by industries you are interested in. Also, be sure to make connections with industry leaders to increase your chances for job opportunities.

2.) Add your website URL

If you don't have a personal website, it's easy to set up. Many hosting companies offer it for free if you host with them, or you can search online for free website templates. If on the other hand you do have a personal website, make sure you showcase your resume and work experience on your website. Be sure to add your website address to your other social media profiles too. Keep it professional like LinkedIn and Twitter, but not your personal Facebook profile. It shows a potential employer that you are connected to social media, and serious about presenting your professional profile in a positive light. This also demonstrates that you know your way around the world of social media, and it also helps if an employer wants to connect with you.

3.) Start connecting with the right people

When researching who to connect with, LinkedIn would be one that I would start with first. Sometimes there are job opportunities that aren't advertised on job boards, and finding contacts at organizations who have openings that are not advertised might take a little work. When putting together a list of prospects, look at individuals who are connected with mutual contacts, and maybe people in the same industry as you, and even people who could recommend you to someone who has a job opening. You can find information about an individual and their role at an organization on LinkedIn by doing job title searches within a geography, or by a specific company name. Once you have identified your list, start connecting with them, follow them on Twitter, and share and repost their tweets as well.

4.) Start a blog

Blogging is a great way to start getting exposure to new contacts, and showcasing your knowledge to a potential employer. If you've never considered starting a blog, you might find that your posts might catch the eye of an important hiring manager or recruiter with an opening that may fit your background and experience.

5.) Keep your profile up to date and accurate

Consistency is key here. If you have multiple social media profiles, all of them should be updated with current information. One of the most important aspects of managing your personal information on social media accounts is to keep that information private. Social media platforms like Facebook, Twitter, LinkedIn, and others allow you to manage what you want to share with friends and the general public. If a potential employer does a search on you, they won't be able to see personal details that you don't want them to see.

If you do want recruiters to find your profile, then you'll probably need to make sure your profile with work history and experience on LinkedIn, Indeed, Monster, Glassdoor, and other job sites where you have resumes is up to date.

Get the word out, and let people know you are looking

When you start connecting with people, make sure you let them know that you are looking for a job. (Provided this doesn't jeopardize your current job). Make sure you are clear about what you are looking for, and set a goal for what you want to achieve with your job search. For example, introductions to hiring managers, referrals, job leads, and sources to where you can apply. You may want to remind friends, contacts and potential employers on a regular basis that you are looking by updated your social media posts about interviews you've had, companies you're researching, and potential employment leads you came across. Don't be shy, ask your friends and contacts to let you know if they come across any potential companies that may be hiring.

15.) Education

Writing the Education Section of Your Resume

The education sections of a resume vary depending on the type and style of resume you are writing. In some cases, it might only be a few lines, while other times it might span more than half a page. Longer education sections are typically used by applicants with advanced academic backgrounds (masters and PhD degrees), or applicants who have taken extensive training and participated in numerous seminars.

What is an education section?

An education section highlights your relevant schooling and academic training. Someone with a substantial work history might incorporate education and work experience into a section that describes how it relates to the job for which you are applying. If you are a currently enrolled college student or a recent graduate, you may want to build this section substantially by highlighting tutoring or teaching positions or other academic achievements.

The education section usually includes information about the following:

- ➢ Name of schools you have attended such as universities, specific trade colleges, junior and community colleges, as well as professional and technical schools
- ➢ Location of schools
- ➢ Date of graduation, (actual or anticipated)
- ➢ Degree(s) earned
- ➢ Grade point average
- ➢ Degree from a college or university
- ➢ Location (city and state)
- ➢ Date of degree
- ➢ Major field of study
- ➢ Minors and areas of special interest, and relevant courses
- ➢ Topic of thesis
- ➢ Language skills

- ➢ GPA
- ➢ Honors

Many people choose to leave out their GPA because it may not be high enough or it may not be relevant for positions for which they are applying. Some companies do request your GPA, and some don't, so you may come across both types of companies in your job search.

Sample:

Bachelor of Science in Industrial Management	May 2000
University of Michigan – Dearborn, Michigan	GPA: 3.5/4.0

Why write an education section?

- ✓ Show employers that your educational and work experience will allow you to do your job efficiently.
- ✓ Highlight your qualifications

Where are educational sections placed on resumes?

Education sections are usually placed in the middle of a resume, somewhere between the objective statement and the activities section. If your educational background is your strongest qualification, then you'll probably want to put it near the top. If you are a recent graduate, this may help a recruiter focus on your education and get a good feel for what positions are best suited for your background. In the case where your experience sections are stronger, then you'll probably want to move your education section below them and highlight these areas.

Building your education section

Depending on how much information you have on your resume, you might want to expand the education section by including some of the content listed below as it applies to your experiences and career goals on your resume or if your educational background is particularly relevant. If you have enough information, you might wish to turn some of the content below into subsections or even into separate sections rather than tuck them under your education section.

SAMPLE CONTENT	
Grade point average (GPA)	**Major GPA:** 3.5/4.0 **Minor GPA:** 3.0/4.0
Major and minor areas of study, concentrations, emphasis or specializations	**Minor:** Business Management **Concentration:** Accounting **Emphasis in:** Corporate Relations

Special projects of mention	**Special Course Project: P&L Business Analysis** Conducted business risk analysis and profitability study. **Thesis:** "Risks of starting a successful business and how to avoid them"
Relevant coursework	**Relevant Coursework:** General Ledger, Journal and Business Ethics
Computer applications	**Computer Literacy:** Microsoft Windows Office Applications – Access, Excel, PowerPoint, Word, and Outlook
Continuing education courses and programs	**Training Workshops**: Business Crisis Management
Academic honors	Bachelor of Science, Accounting (Magna Cum Laude) Graduated with distinction
Academic Funding or Loans	B.S. in Accounting Full Scholarship
Professional Certifications	APICS – CPIM, Project Management Inc. – PMP

Targeting Your Audience

In order to make your education section stand out, you need to know what content will be most valued by the hiring company. You can get a good sense for which of the educational qualifications are most relevant by analyzing job postings and reviewing company literature as part of your job search.

You may tailor your education section in four ways:

1. **Include only your most relevant educational content**. Based on your career goals and the qualifications, you might include only certain information. For example, if you have a specialized degree and you took courses that relate to the work you are applying for, you might want to list the coursework. However, if your degree is in a discipline that employers will likely know, then you may omit this section.

2. **Emphasize content and placement.** Most readers are drawn to the top section headings, so you may choose to put your most impressive and relevant educational experiences in their own sections or subsections, or near the top of a section. For instance, if you have

some special skills, you may choose to put this information in its own section rather than list under education.

3. **List most relevant school work first.** Many use reverse chronological order, but you also have the option of placing your most relevant educational experiences first.

4. **Use a mix of education and work experience,** You can highlight your educational experience in the foreground and relevant work experience in the background. For example, if you have a background in an academic field, then this may fit well. If you have some work experience, then you may want to highlight work first, then education at the bottom.

Education Section Format Examples

Regardless of the format you use, you need an education section on your resume. In the education section, highlight continuing education or other on-the-job training.

When writing this section, keep the layout consistent, for example listing the college first, then the degree, or vice versa). Start with the highest degree you have earned and work backwards. Add distinctions, awards, and extracurricular work.

If you did not complete a college degree but are working toward the completion of one, mention the relevant coursework you have taken and include the expected completion date. If high school is your highest degree completed, list it. Otherwise, it does not need to be mentioned.

Education

Example 1:   **University of Southern California** – Burbank, California 1998
Master of Science, Operations Management GPA 3.7/4.0
Areas of emphasis: Industrial Management

University of California, Los Angeles – Burbank, California 1992
Bachelor of Science, Industrial Engineering GPA 3.95/4.0
Exchange Student Program during senior year in Germany
Fluent in German and Swedish

Example 2:   **University of Southern California** – Burbank, California 1998
Master of Science, Operations Management GPA 3.7/4.0
Areas of emphasis: Industrial Management

University of California - Los Angeles – Burbank, California 1992
Bachelor of Science, Industrial Engineering GPA 3.95/4.0
Exchange Student Program during senior year in Germany
Fluent in German and Swedish

APICS – CPIM Certification 1995
National Computer Learning Centers – Web Development training
Certified in: .Net, Visual Basic, Java, HTML, PHP and MySql

Letter of Recommendation

Letters of Recommendation for Job-Searching

Letters of recommendation act as substitutes for work references in that they neatly sum up a previous or current employer's perspective and allow prospective employers to avoid interrogating references about your strengths and weaknesses. Additionally, they are also a great advantage for the job seeker, because they offer credible evidence of past accomplishments and abilities.

If you have been laid off but left the company on good terms, a letter of recommendation will provide prospective employers with a credible account of why you had to leave the company.

Letters of Recommendation for Applications

In the academic world, undergraduate and graduate-school applications require two or three letters of recommendation, depending on whether you are applying to an academic program or professional degree from a business or law school. These letters should come from former or current professors, employers, or supervisors who are familiar with your work and performance.

16.) Power Words

Using these action words in your resume could mean the difference between getting an interview and not getting called at all. You might not use these words every day, so remember to spell check your resume.

Achieved	Accelerated	Accomplished	Administered	Advised
Allocated	Analyzed	Answered	Applied	Appeared
Appointed	Appraised	Approved	Arranged	Assessed
Assigned	Assisted	Attained	Audited	Augmented
Awarded	Bought	Briefed	Broadened	Budgeted
Built	Calculated	Captured	Cataloged	Centralized
Changed	Closed	Collected	Combined	Completed
Composed	Conceived	Conceptualized	Conducted	Consolidated
Consulted	Controlled	Converted	Coordinated	Corrected
Created	Delivered	Dealt	Decreased	Decided
Defined	Demonstrated	Designed	Determined	Developed
Devised	Diagnosed	Directed	Discussed	Distributed
Documented	Earned	Edited	Effected	Engineered
Ensured	Established	Estimated	Evaluated	Expedited
Experienced	Experimented	Explained	Extended	Expanded
Filed	Filled	Financed	Focused	Founded
Forecast	Formed	Formulated	Founded	Gathered
Granted	Helped	Generated	Guided	Identified
Implemented	Improved	Incorporated	Increased	Indexed
Influenced	Innovated	Inspected	Installed	Insured
Interviewed	Invented	Invested	Investigated	Involved
Issued	Identified	Implemented	Improvised	Increased
Initiated	Instructed	Instituted	Joined	Kept

69

Interpreted	Introduced	Launched	Lectured	Led
Licensed	Listed	Logged	Maintained	Managed
Marketed	Matched	Measured	ediated	Modernized
Monitored	Negotiated	Observed	Obtained	Operated
Organized	Oversaw	Performed	Planned	Prepared
Presented	Processed	Promoted	Participated	Performed
Persuaded	Planned	Prepared	Presented	Processed
Procured	Programmed	Projected	Promoted	Proposed
Provided	Published	Purchased	Qualified	Questioned
Raised	Ranked	Rated	Realized	Received
Recommended	Reconciled	Recorded	Recruited	Redesigned
Reduced	Regulated	Rehabilitated	Related	Reorganized
Repaired	Replaced	Simplified	Sold	Solved
Sorted	Specified	Staffed	Streamlined	Strengthened
Stretched	Structured	Studied	Submitted	Replied
Reported	Represented	Researched	Resolved	Responded
Restored	Revamped	Reviewed	Revise	Saved
Scheduled	Selected	Served	Serviced	Set
Set Up	Shaped	Shared	Showed	Summarized
Superseded	Supervised	Surveyed	Systematized	Tackled
Targeted	Taught	Terminated	Tested	Took
Toured	Traced	Tracked	Traded	Trained
Transferred	Transcribed	Transformed	Translated	Transported
Traveled	Treated	Trimmed	Tripled	Turned
Tutored	Umpired	Uncovered	Understood	Understudied
Unified	Unraveled	Updated	Upgraded	Used
Utilized	Verbalized	Verified	Visited	Waged
Weighed	Widened	Won	Worked	Wrote

Examples of how to use these power words:

- Coordinated efforts...
- Dealt directly with customers on a daily basis...
- Delivered high standards of...
- Boost company productivity...

- Increase efficiency…
- Improved team performance…
- Reduced overhead costs…
- Successfully implemented…
- Successfully increased…
- Reported to…
- Managed and motivated…
- Responsible for…
- Successfully led…
- Established process flow…

17.) Cover Letters

How To Prepare An Effective Cover Letter

The cover letter is an important part of your job search campaign. Truth be told, many employers will not even look at your resume if you do not have a cover letter attached. You can also strike out if your cover letter is poorly written or hard to understand. If your cover letter is not read, chances are your resume won't get read either. It's hard to get an interview when no one reads your resume. Therefore, give the same careful consideration and attention to the preparation of cover letters as you gave to your resume.

There are two types of cover letters you might use in your job search:

Letter of Application or Response to an Advertisement: This type of letter is used when you are responding to a specific advertised opening. You should show how your skills and qualifications fit the requirements of the position.

Letter of Inquiry: This type of letter is used when you are contacting an individual or organization to ask about possible openings. You should focus on broader occupational or organizational requirements to demonstrate how your qualifications match the work environment or how your skills can help the company meet its needs.

Whichever type of cover letter you send, it will say a lot about you as a professional and as a prospective employee. Your cover letter should be a clear demonstration of your written communication skills and relevant industry experience, as well as your ability to convince and persuade the reader that you would be an asset to the organization. This means you'll have to prepare a new letter for each company. Research the particular needs and requirements of the organization and position for which you are applying.

You must compose a letter that communicates your value in a concise and professional manner. The cover letter guidelines and sample paragraphs that follow should help you achieve these goals.

General Guidelines and Suggestions for Preparing Cover Letters

1. **Write clearly and simply**. Keep it simple and avoid jargon. Keep it short and sweet by saying what you have to say directly.

2. **Keep it brief**. A one-page letter comprising three to four paragraphs should suffice. Your cover letter should never be more than one page long.

3. **Show what you can do for the reader, not what you want the reader to do for you**. Keep the focus on your qualifications as they relate to the position you are seeking.

4. **Make mention of one or two specific accomplishments or strengths**. Demonstrate your expertise or proficiency and make the reader want to know more about you, then refer the reader to your resume for more information.

5. **Make sure your letters are easy to read**. Keep to the point but demonstrate that you have sound business-writing principles in your communications.

6. **Compose high quality, error-free copy**. Be sure to proofread your cover letter carefully. Use the same font and pitch used in your resume, and make your letter look as much like your resume as possible.

7. **Whenever possible, address your letter to a specific person and include their title, if known**. If you don't have a name but do know the company, call the main switchboard or human resources department and ask for the name of the human resources manager, the name of the person handling the opening, or the person in charge of the department where the position will be located. If you can't find a name, go to the "careers" section of the company's website you should be able to get the name of the human resources or recruiting person. It's not advisable to use a generic salutation like "Dear Sir or Madam" or "To Whom It May Concern." It's too informal for the reader.

8. **Use high-quality stationary and envelopes.** Use the same paper as your resume and purchase matching envelopes.

9. **Be honest**. You should be able to back up what you say with evidence and specific examples from your experience.

10. **Be positive in your tone, attitude, choice of words and expectations**. Convey your self-confidence, enthusiasm, and professionalism.

11. **Be sure to sign your letter** using your full name as typed. Use a high-quality pen with black or blue ink, and be sure your signature is legible.

12. **Close by stating what action you will be taking as a follow-up to your letter**. This takes the burden off the reader and also gives you more control over the process.

BASIC ELEMENTS OF THE COVER LETTER

Name
Address
City, State, Zip code
Phone Number
E-Mail

Date of Letter
Reader's Name
Reader's Title
Name of Company
Company Address

Salutation: Use the reader's title and last name if available (e.g., Dear Mr. Jones or Dear Ms. Jones:). In this case you want to be formal, so don't use a first name unless you know the individual well and are certain this is acceptable. If you do not have a contact name, use the title (e.g., Dear Operations Manager:). If you're not sure or don't have the contact person's name, and don't know if the person is a male or female, use the full name with no title (e.g., Dear Taylor Jones).

Opening Paragraph: Make it clear what your message and intention is in this letter. State the name, the position or type of work you are applying for and mention how you heard of the job opening.

Middle Paragraphs: Describe your strengths as they relate to the position you are seeking. Mention a few accomplishments that illustrate your proficiency and effectiveness. The idea is to create interest on the reader's part and show how your skills and qualifications can be of value to the organization. You don't want to reiterate the same thing in your cover letter that's in your resume. Instead, refer the reader to your enclosed resume for more detail on your qualifications and experience.

Closing Paragraph: Restate your interest in the position or organization and your desire for an in-person meeting. This will pave the way for the interview by indicating the action or steps you will take to initiate a meeting. Lastly, express your appreciation for the reader's time and consideration for this position.

Sincerely,

Your full name
Enclosure

SAMPLE COVER LETTER
(LETTER OF INQUIRY)

ROBERT P. JONES
1234 Main Street
Small Town, Statesville 54321
(123) 456-6789

(Current Date)

Mary Peterson, Manager
Accounting Department
XYZ Company
10 Dear Park Drive
Omaha, Nebraska 68102

Dear Ms. Peterson:

I am writing to introduce myself to your organization, at the request of Mr. William Danielson of ABC Company. He has indicated to me that you have a position open for an advertising copywriter.

As you can see in the enclosed resume, I have a strong background in print advertising, combined with over seven years work experience at a full-service advertising agency. My role as a copywriter covers print, video and other electronic media. I have developed strong technical, analytical and problem-solving skills through the successful completion of a major project involving the creation, assembly and copywriting campaign for our national furniture franchise client. As part of your team, I believe that I could make a significant and valuable contribution to future projects within your organization, as well as other challenges that you may be facing.

I would appreciate the opportunity to discuss how my experience and education would play an important role in addressing your needs. I will follow up you within the next few days to talk about the possibility of arranging an interview. Thank you for your time and consideration.

Sincerely,

Robert P. Jones

Enclosure

SAMPLE COVER LETTER
(RESPONSE TO ADVERTISEMENT)

Dear Human Resources Manager:

I am applying for the position of Accounting Manager, as advertised on [name of career website]. With over seven years' experience as a corporate accountant, I believe I could make a significant contribution in helping ABC Corporation address internal and external cost issues, and other goals and objectives.

As an example of my most recent accomplishments, I conducted a corporate-wide assessment of current operating costs. I eliminated redundant costs, balanced budgets for two departments and increased financial awareness for the company's future purchases. I believe that my expertise in these areas would be of particular value in meeting the challenges of your organization.

SAMPLE LETTER
(LETTER OF WITHDRAWAL DURING THE JOB SEARCH)

I am writing to inform you that I am withdrawing my application for the marketing analyst position we discussed last week. As I indicated in our meeting, I have a strong interest in speaking to clients in the metropolitan Atlanta area. I have been exploring several career opportunities in that area. Earlier this week, I was offered and, after careful consideration, have accepted a position with an advertising agency in the Atlanta area.

I want to express my sincere appreciation for the time you spent considering my candidacy and the interest you showed in my background during our interview. I truly enjoyed meeting you and learning more about ABC Company and the exciting projects you have planned.

SAMPLE LETTER
(LETTER OF REJECTION AFTER A JOB OFFER)

Thank you for offering me the position of marketing analyst with your organization. I appreciate your confidence in my ability to handle the many challenges of this position.

The position offered is indeed a challenging one that would make good use of my experience and educational background. It certainly would have allowed me the opportunity to enhance and strengthen my overall skills and qualifications. However, after careful consideration, I have decided to pursue other career endeavors that will match my long-range career goals more closely.

SAMPLE LETTER
(LETTER OF ACCEPTANCE AFTER A JOB OFFER)

As discussed in our telephone conversation yesterday, I am pleased to accept your employment offer for the accounting manager position. The position is an excellent match with my skills and experience, and I am confident that I can make a significant contribution to your organization.

As we agreed, the start date will be August 6, at which time I will complete the necessary paperwork and attend your new employee orientation. I understand that the starting salary will be $5,000 per month, not including bonuses and full benefits.

TOP 18 COVER LETTER MISTAKES TO AVOID

1. Comparisons and clichés: Avoid overused clichés because such expressions distract from your letter's purpose. You want to showcase your most impressive skills and accomplishments.

2. Unrelated or unrealistic career goals: Tailor your cover letter to the specific position for which you are applying. Hiring managers are only interested in what you can do for the company, not what you hope to accomplish for yourself. Your letter should convey a genuine interest in the position and how you will fulfill your duties. **Example:** "I am very interested in this executive assistant position, and I am confident in my ability to make a long-term contribution to your staff."

3. General form letters: This is mass mailing in which you send a general form letter to a large number of employers. This is not recommended because this approach does not allow you to personalize each application. Every cover letter you write should be tailored to the position you are seeking and demonstrate both your commitment to a specific industry and particular employer. Mass mailings might indicate to a hiring manager that you are not truly interested in joining his or her organization.

4. Inappropriate stationery: White and ivory are the only acceptable paper colors for a cover letter. Stay away from other so-called creative colors, like pinks and blues. Use standard office stationery, and avoid clear or transparent typing paper or personal stationery.

5. Wasting space: Cover letters are generally just a few paragraphs long, and every word of every sentence should be directly related to your purpose for writing. In other words, if you are applying for a position as an engineer, include only the skills and experience that apply to that field. Any other irrelevant information weakens your application.

6. Incorrect or erroneous company information: Verify the accuracy of any company information that you mention in your cover letter. If you haven't researched the company, don't exaggerate. Saying something like: "I know about your company" or "I am familiar with your products" signal to an employer that you haven't done your homework. Be specific when citing information about a company.

7. Personal photos: This is the no-no you most want to avoid. Adding a photo to your cover letter or even resume is a sure way of eliminating you from consideration for the position advertised. One of the reasons is you might remind the interviewer of someone he or she does not like.

8. Mentioning shortcomings: This is a big mistake because you're emphasizing your flaws rather than your strengths. For example, avoid statements like, "Although I don't have related experience, I remain very interested in the store manager position," or "I'm not qualified for this position, but I always wanted to work in the dry cleaning field." Instead, emphasize your strengths, including valuable skills, related experience, and company knowledge.

9. "Amusing" anecdotes: If you want serious consideration from a prospective employer, your cover letter should present a serious, professional tone. Let's imagine you're in an interview setting. Since you do not know your interviewer, you would not joke with him or her until you have determined what demeanor is appropriate. Likewise, when writing to a potential employer you never met, you should remain professional.

10. Misrepresentation: At any point of a job search, NEVER ever misrepresent yourself. Erroneous claims in a cover letter or resume could be grounds for dismissal as soon as the inaccuracy is discovered. Stick to the facts. You are selling your skills and accomplishments in your cover letter. If you achieve something, say so, and put it in the best possible light. Don't hold back or be modest.

11. Missing resume: Don't forget to enclose all the materials you refer to in your cover letter. Failure to enclose case studies or other materials is not only a disappointment, but a fatal oversight. Employers don't have time to remind you of your mistake; they will move on to the next application.

12. Personal information: Do not include your age, weight, height, marital status, race, religion, or any other personal information unless you feel that it directly pertains to the position that you're seeking. If you are applying for an athletic sports team, height and weight may be important to include. Similarly, you should list your personal interests and hobbies only if they are directly relevant to the type of job you are seeking.

13. Choice of pronouns: Your cover letter requires a thorough discussion of your qualifications. Although some applicants might choose the third person ("he or she") as a creative approach to presenting their qualifications, potential employers sometimes find this disconcerting. In general, using the first person is preferable.

14. Demanding statements: Your cover letter should demonstrate what you can could do for an employer, not what he or she can do for you. Instead of saying, "I am looking for an opportunity in which I will be adequately challenged and compensated," say, "I am confident that I could make a significant contribution to your organization, specifically by expanding your customer base in the Midwest region and implementing incentive programs for new accounts."

15. Gimmicks: Sending a home video or a singing telegram to replace the conventional cover letter might seem tempting. No matter how creative these ideas may sound, the majority of employers will be more impressed with a simple, well-crafted letter. In the worst-case scenario, gimmicks can even work against you, eliminating you from consideration. Avoid taking such big risks. Most hiring decisions are based on qualifications, not gimmicks.

16. Corrections: Provide pertinent information in your cover letter. But if you forget to communicate something to your addressee, you can easily retype the letter in Microsoft Word. Including a supplementary note, either typed or handwritten, will be viewed as unprofessional or, worse yet, lazy.

17. Omitted signature: As obvious as this might sound, don't forget to sign your name at the close of your cover letter. Far too many people have a typed name, but no signature. An employer might interpret this oversight as care- lessness. Your signature allows you the chance to personalize your letter, and remember to always sign your name neatly in blue or black ink.

18. Typographical errors: It is very easy to make mistakes in your letters, especially when you are writing many in succession. But it is also very easy for a hiring manager to reject any cover letter that contains errors, even those that seem minor at first glance. Here are a few common mistakes to watch out for when proofreading your letter:

- ✓ Misspelling the hiring contact's name or title in the address, the greet- ing, or on the envelope.
- ✓ Forgetting to change the name of the organization you're applying to each time it appears in your application, especially in the body of the letter.
- ✓ Indicating application for one position and mentioning a different posi- tion in the body of the letter. It's easy to make a mistake if you cut and paste the body of the text and just add the new contact information.

18.) Job Hunting and Career Counseling

Helpful Networking Tips

1. Brainstorm for Contacts

Everyone you know could serve as a potential contact. Don't limit yourself to people who could clearly help you out. Friendly, accessible people in unrelated fields often have contacts they would be happy to share with you. It can be extremely helpful to reach out to your network of work or volunteer-activities contacts. Here are some suggestions to get you started:

Family members	Religious leaders
Relatives	Community members
Neighbors	Business executives
Professors	Non-profit directors
Alumni	Your physician
Your dry cleaners	Your hair dresser
Former co-workers	Members of professional organizations
Public relations officials	Friends in public office

2. Where the Contacts Are: Tried and True Places to Network

Local alumni association	Conventions
Class reunions	Club meetings
Cocktail parties	Internet career communities
Fundraisers	Volunteer opportunities
Business conferences	Continuing education classes

3. Be Prepared

Networking is a valuable tool which has its rewards. When you are at a networking function, you should be relaxed and honest, but don't wing it. You should be thinking about why you are there, and what it is you want to accomplish. You should approach networking opportunities with a game plan. Before you confidently stroll into the conference room, a dinner party, or group event, do your homework. Find out who will be there, or do your best to list who you think will probably be present. Then decide who you would most like to meet. When you have your list of potential contacts, thoroughly research their work and backgrounds and brainstorm some questions and conversational statements that reflect your research. And finally, think critically about your goals for the networking function. What information do you want to walk away with? What do you want to convey to the people you meet?

You must also be flexible and adapt to situations you didn't plan to confront. One example of adapting is working under a set of daily routine responsibilities, and then on short notice, adding additional responsibilities that you may not be ready to handle or may need additional training.

4. Creative Networking

This approach should be a very fluid one in which you feel comfortable speaking to anyone in the room regardless if they are a CEO of a large organization, or a retail store manager. Remember to treat everyone with respect because you never know who you will meet and how important they might be to your career. While it may have been sheer luck that you bumped into a respectable CEO, your savvy approach to networking can turn a casual exchange into a pivotal moment in your career path. Always be ready to make a contact and exchange business cards.

5. Following Up

After you meet with a contact, it is essential to write a thank-you note. Mention in the note that you appreciate the time and help the employer spent with you. Everyone likes to feel appreciated. In addition to an immediate follow-up after a meeting or conversation, keep in touch with your contacts. They may think of you if an opportunity comes up, and they will be more likely to pass your name along to others looking for qualified professionals.

6. Remember Those Who Helped You

If you want your phone calls and e-mails to be returned, remember to call and write back the people who contact you. If you want big shots to make time for you, make yourself available to others you might be able to help out. The higher up you climb up the corporate ladder, the more you'll find that everyone knows everyone else. If you're impolite, rude, or condescending, you'll quickly build an infamous reputation. Remember: The people who seem little now will one day be running companies and making decisions. If you treat them with kindness and respect when they're green, they'll remember and return the favor later.

7. Stay Organized

Keep a record of your networking activities by noting your contacts in a spreadsheet, Microsoft Word document, or on your tablet. These lists should include contacts' names, addresses, phone numbers, companies, job titles, and notes on how you met them and what you talked about.

Job Search Frequently Asked Questions

What are the advantages and disadvantages of taking on temporary jobs while looking for full-time work?

There are a lot of advantages to this approach, especially since more and more companies are hiring temporary professionals in the middle and senior-levels. These assignments give you a nice "working while I find the ideal job" option. Working temporary jobs gives you a chance to network more and de-velop new skills. If the employer likes your work, it might evolve into a full-time position with the company. The downside is that you could end up working on your job search after working hours.

How truthful should you be when answering interview questions?

Be as truthful as possible. However, you can be honest without volunteering information that could work against you. If you're asked how you would handle a particular assignment, you can truthfully answer, "I think I could handle that problem very well," even if you have doubts. But misrepresenting specific facts about your background that can be verified is another thing altogether. Small misrepresentations can cost you dearly, casting doubt on everything else you've said during the interview and on your resume.

What's the best response if you feel you're being treated unfairly by an interviewer?

The first thing you must do is to determine whether or not the interviewer's behavior is deliberately designed to put you under pressure. Some interview-ers will test you to see how you respond to pressure if you're hired. Such tests aren't common, but it's possible that the job requires you to keep your cool under pressure. But if you're dealing with a person who is being outright nasty, it doesn't pay to blow your lid. However, it is appropriate to comment if the interviewer's remarks become blatant, which rarely happens.

How do you overcome the "you're overqualified" objection?

Have you ever heard the dreadful "We think you're overqualified for this position" response? The interviewer is likely concerned about whether you're truly interested in this job, whether you will be motivated to do your best, or whether you'll be satisfied with a compensation package that is probably lower than what you're accustomed. Rather than getting upset or arguing the point with the interviewer, emphasize that you are enthusiastic and motivated about the job, and that the salary drop is not an issue. Stress the fact that the firm is getting a value-added asset by hiring you.

What do you do if you're too young?

Don't put any dates on your education. List experiences like golf caddying, babysitting, and mowing lawns in your summary section to imply additional experience. The goal here is to keep from telling your age, which gives potential employers an excuse to discriminate against you.

What if you have the wrong kind of experience?

Explain what you have learned in your past experience that might apply to the new position. For example, if you worked in a dry cleaning store, break down the process of how garments come in, get tagged and are separated in specific bins and assigned to either dry cleaning or laundry. This illustrates to the interviewer that you know the entire process from start to finish. This also gives the interviewer confidence in your abilities to do the job. You should use an entirely different language to interest a technical recruiter for an engineering job. If you were a design engineer, you might list reviewing engineering drawings, creating designs for parts on Computer Aided Design software, making changes to existing drawings, and approving drawings.

What do you do if you have the wrong degree?

If you have a degree in nursing and now want a job in financial services, omit the major. Instead feature the coursework related to your target field.

What do you do if you have date gaps?

Date gaps in your resume will raise red flags, and recruiters will pick up on the gaps quickly. The reality is that most people have gaps in their resumes. If asked about the gaps, don't lie, but explain it in a positive light. Explain that you were on maternity leave and wanted to start a family, or that you joined the military and were away from your job for a tour or two.

19.) Short- and Long-Term Goals

A good recruiter will ask a candidate to discuss their goals, which serves several purposes. The interviewer is trying to find out if the position and company are a good fit for the candidate. The interviewer will also be looking at the candidate's motivation and sincere interest in the position and company. Expect questions that will reveal your attitude, motivation, attentiveness, and organized thought. The interviewer wants to know if the candidate is just looking for a "stop over" filler job to pay the rent and other bills instead of seeking growth within the company.

Should I change careers?

Many business-industry journals report that a number of Americans wish they could change their jobs. Those who take the initiative and plan their job search are one step closer to finding the job they enjoy. But give your current employer the benefit of a doubt. Ask if they can make changes that will satisfy your needs at your current job.

Before you rush to revise your resume for that career change, review these questions and answers.

1.) What is it about my current position that I like?
2.) What is it about my current position that I dislike?
3.) Is there anything I can do to change or improve current working conditions?
4.) If I am able to make these changes or improve these conditions, do I still want to stay in this job and industry?
5.) Can you translate your skills into your job function?
6.) Are you in an industry or occupation that has limited growth opportunities or advancement?
7.) Is compensation for your type of occupation low or not competitive in the marketplace?
8.) Are you working in an environment that does not utilize your full potential?
9.) Are there any continuing education/training opportunities in your workplace?

Answering these questions will give you an idea whether you need to reassess your skills to move on to a new career or add additional skills to improve your current job and increase your compensation. Here are a few scenarios that may help you decide one way or the other:

1. I feel like I'm not accomplishing anything important at work, it's because:

(a) There's a big gap between what I feel I could be doing and the job description for a typical employee in my field.
(b) My current job doesn't allow me the help/resources or flexibility to accomplish what I want.

2. When I first started looking for a job:

(a) This type of work was hard to find in the specific field that I was trained for, and I had to settle for my current job because it paid reasonably well.
(b) I easily found work in my chosen field, but have since become unhappy with my current position.

3. I look forward to time off because:

(a) I have a chance to spend time on things I enjoy.
(b) I get to relax and not think about e-mail and phone calls.

4. The hardest part of my job is:

(a) Translating my skills into productive tasks that actually relate to my work.
(b) Coping with either too few or too many challenges.

5. My field of work:

(a) Has drastically changed within the past few years. My role within the company when I was hired is very different than what I'm actually doing now.
(b) Is pretty much the same as it was when I first started; however, with some continuing education, I could update my skills and possibly get a promotion and a raise.

6. The number of opportunities for continuing education at work are:

a) Very limited. I've exhausted all options for upward growth and career advancement; although I wish I could do more, like attend workshops and conferences. This would definitely allow me professional growth.

What Your Answers Reveal

Mostly A's: A change might be just what you need to rejuvenate your career. What you're expressing is not just unhappiness with your environment, but a fundamental need to pursue opportunities that your current field cannot offer. The next step is to assess what skills you want to utilize in another occupation. If you've made the mistake of settling once, don't do it again. Most importantly, don't confuse your excitement of a newly discovered field as making it a fit for you. When the glitz wears off, you don't want to find yourself in the same position you're in now.

Mostly B's: Your career isn't the problem, but your current job might not be offering you what you need in terms of challenges and responsibilities. On the other hand, you might have too much on your plate and need to take a break. If your financial situation allows you some time off, take it. Chances are, you will return to work more relaxed and ready to do your best, or you can attend some workshops and seminars that will provide you with the competitive edge you need to play a more proactive role in your workplace.

Contacting Hiring Managers

1. Always ask to meet the hiring manager

The goal is to get hired. You must convince an employer that you have what the employer is looking for and that you can do the work.

Question: What's the easiest way to meet the person who can hire you?
Answer: Simply find out who the hiring manager is and ask them to meet with you.

But this is easier said than done. A lot of people are not comfortable calling and making such inquiries. Like it or not, this is what you need to do to get an interview. Take a proactive approach and make the follow-up phone call after submitting your resume instead of waiting for the phone to ring after submitting an ad.

HOT TIP: Use your network of personal and professional contacts to get the name of the hiring manager. Next, request an informal meeting with the hiring manager.

2. Sending your resume to many people via e-mail

It's getting harder to send an e-mail to a friend or colleague without your e-mail message getting scrutinized by companies who install spam filters.

Sending mass e-mails can be tricky because e-mail servers classify them as spam. You could be put on a "Black List," or a group of e-mail addresses to notify internet service providers or others who have an interest in this list that you send spam to people.

Avoid using generic keywords in the subject line. Be specific about the position for which you are applying, including position title and any related advertisement ID numbers.

We will talk about resume distribution services later in the book.

3. Use the interview to prove you can do the job

Remember, you must prove to a hiring manager that you are qualified for the job. What better way than to actually do the job at the interview?

Examples:

- ✓ A sales person could bring a book of 50 potential customers to the interview.
- ✓ A systems engineer could uncover some advanced computer systems networking flaws or infrastructure problems, then propose solutions.
- ✓ A nurse could explain a process flow in triage that shortens the wait times for patients in the Emergency Room.

Each of the above real-life examples resulted in a job offer. Use your next interview to actually do the job. While other candidates are learning about the company or asking questions, take the initiative and set yourself apart.

What are Real-World Accomplishments?

One of the things that employers will look at when they size you up in the interview process is to see if you are worth the investment; essentially, if you will pay off in the short- or long-term. Let's look at both sides of the accomplishment coin.

Accomplishments

1. Increasing the company's bottom line;
2. Streamlining processes and procedures;
3. Projects successfully completed;
4. Decreasing direct & indirect costs; and
5. Professional certifications and licensure.

Not Accomplishments

1. Daily responsibilities that are included in your job description;
2. Regular attendance at work;
3. Getting along with other co-workers;
4. Working full-time while taking evening college classes; and
5. Volunteer or community service work that has a direct bearing on your job search.

20.) Resume Databases and What Job Seekers Should Know

Is your resume safe once you post it on a career job board?

After you post your resume, it is usually out of your control. Generally, job sites do not have the ability to track or control how a recruiter or employer uses your resume after it has been downloaded. Most sites are pretty good about watching for problems. These practices are frowned upon and enforced by the terms of use agreements with employers and recruiters. But keep in mind there are risks involved in posting a resume in a database.

Watch out for job scams

The job offer you see might not be for a real job. After you post your resume, you may be contacted by someone trying to scam you with a fake job offer. This is becoming a very serious problem in online job searching. Here are some red flags that should alert you to these scams.

- ✓ Have you been asked for your social security number?
- ✓ Have you been asked to scan your ID or driver's license and send it in?
- ✓ Have you been asked to do a money transfer as part of your duties?
- ✓ Have you been asked to respond to e-mails that describe high-paying jobs that require you to sign up for an eBay, PayPal or Western Union account, and to transfer monies in any one of these modes?

General job descriptions usually don't offer much of an opportunity

After posting your resume, you should start getting responses. Be wise and selective about offers, because not all offers are worth your time. If you get an e-mail that asks you to send a resume to a new email address or to "update" your resume on a new job site, think twice, especially when you do not see a credible job being offered with a verifiable company. Some companies get you to send a new resume just so they can put it in their resume database.

Resume posting options

You have a few options when you post your resume. You can do an anony-mous posting, which lets you hide your contact information or e-mail address when you post a resume. This resume posting option allows you to control who contacts you. You can also get selective and only post information about your background that specific employers are looking for. Unfortunately, few job seekers take advantage of this option. You can also post your resume on-line for the world to see. This method is normally used by job seekers who are not working and would like to explore opportunities by a variety of companies.

Some resume databases are better than others

You'll find a variety of resume databases online, and some that serve specific industries or occupations. Before you post your resume to any database, read the site's privacy policy. This will tell you if your information is being protected and how your information is being used. Some of the better job boards will state that they do not sell your private information to marketing companies. If you post to boards that sell your information to marketing companies, you will probably start getting bombarded with spam soon after. If the website does not have a privacy policy posted, you should be especially cautious about posting a resume to that website.

How frequently should you check the website where you have your re-sume posted?

You should pay attention to how long a resume website says it will keep or store your resume. Many job seekers overlook this. Some sites state their re-tention time in their privacy policy, usually between one and six months, after which the site will delete your resume. Without specific written statements about how long your resume may be kept, your resume can be searched for years. Most job seekers do not want resumes circulating after they have se-cured a job, so check to make sure there is a limited posting time before you post a resume. If you are not sure about how long it will stay on the website, contact them to ask. You should have the option to delete or change anything on your online profile at any time.

Keep good records of your job search

Make sure you keep a record of where you have posted your resume online. Include in that record all e-mail correspondence and any online profiles you compiled. You should print out a copy of the posted job advertisement, so you can refer to it if you are called for a phone or in-person interview. Don't be in a hurry to delete old correspondence from your record. Some employers keep resumes on file for a period of six to 12 months in case new positions come up.

Different e-mail addresses for website posting advertisements

There are a few good reasons why you should have different e-mail address-es. You should set up an address for responding to "blind" career opportu-nities, or those from companies that post ads without their company infor-mation. In essence, you are doing the same thing. Using an e-mail address that you can cancel anytime is a good way to keep your information private. Expect to be inundated with spam, so don't give out your name, phone num-ber, or home address when setting up these e-mail accounts.

Two important things to omit when applying online

You may end up going to quite a few career websites, and you will probably create resume profiles that can be searched by recruiting firms and employ-ers directly. Never volunteer your social security number or references on any websites. These can be furnished at a later phase of the interview process.

For example:
1.) You can furnish references only when you have a potential offer on the table.
2.) You can supply your social security number only when you have ac-cepted a position and have established a start date, or when you have already started your new job as part of the employee orientation.

21.) Career Counseling – Marketing Your Talents to the Job Market

A lot of people apply for jobs not knowing if they are a good fit for the position or even if they have the skills necessary for the position. Even before you decide to do your job search, it's important to understand your strengths and weaknesses.

You won't get a second chance to make a good first impression, no matter how awful your first impression may be. In this world of increasing competition, there will always be another candidate waiting in the wings to take over where you fell short, so take your job search as seriously as you would an important work project. Set clear objectives and goals around your job search. Research prospective employers and familiarize yourself with the specific positions you seek. Employers want to see you take initiative and be proactive.

How to Select the Right Position

Even before you start preparing for your interview, research your prospective company so you can set appropriate expectations for the position. Before you put your best foot forward, you need to perform the following research:

- ✓ Match the job requirements to your experience.
- ✓ Research the company, products, services, and current and past performance.
- ✓ What performance criteria will you be measured against?
- ✓ To whom will you be reporting, and what is his or her work style?
- ✓ What opportunities are there for advancement in the company?
- ✓ What are the responsibilities that are involved in the job?

In the course of your research, you should ask yourself how closely you match the job requirements. Example:

- ✓ Are you capable of performing the job?
- ✓ Do you have the relevant experience and ability?
- ✓ Do you match the organization goals and corporate culture?
- ✓ Will the job be challenging enough for you?
- ✓ Can you see yourself getting promotions and making advancements in the company based on your career aspirations?

If after performing this task you feel strongly that this is the position you desire, then the hard part lies ahead.

Proper Career Planning – Getting to Know Yourself

Most people have difficulty communicating what it is they are looking for in a job. Many find it even harder to find a position that will give them satisfaction and the necessary motivation to perform well. You can overcome these difficulties by taking the time to evaluate your circumstances in addition to your needs. You should think about all aspects of the job taking into account the following considerations:

- ✓ What factors about the organization do you like? Dislike?
- ✓ Do you work well with your manager and colleagues?
- ✓ What have been your achievements thus far in your career, and what ambitions have yet to be fulfilled?
- ✓ What do you like and dislike about your present position?
- ✓ Where is the new position based, and do you have any travel restrictions?
- ✓ What hours do you work, and do they affect your quality of life?

Putting Your Job Search in High Gear

You might be faced with an unproductive job search in a down economy. This can make your search a little depressing and might delay your eventual success. Don't get discouraged. Maintain a positive attitude, because you do have something of value to offer. Some of the things that I've heard people say is:

- ✓ "I've sent out hundreds of resumes and I haven't found a job yet."
- ✓ "Why apply? Chances are there's an internal candidate who will get the job anyway."
- ✓ "I never see jobs listed for someone with my _____." (Fill in the blank: experience, major, skills.)

Resumes That Work

Using the same approach you've always used will probably produce the same results. If this is the case, it's time for a new strategy. Some suggestions:

- ✓ Target your resumes and cover letters to your selected readers.
- ✓ Research the companies to which you are applying so you can be prepared. Your resume and cover letter should read as if they are meant specifically for your target employer.
- ✓ Find out the hiring manager's name and address your letter to them directly. Try not to be informal. This is a great opportunity to tell the employer you are the right person for the job.
- ✓ Have you covered all your core skills, along with experience, accomplishments and education?
- ✓ Believe it or not, many available jobs are never advertised in your local newspapers. So, look at all available vehicles of advertising for your job search including networking, traditional, and non-traditional methods.

Avoid Simple Mistakes That Keep You Unemployed

1.) Make sure you have the right contact information on your resume so potential employers have a way to get a hold of you.
2.) If a potential employer will be contacting by phone, make sure you leave a professional message on your answering machine without music in the background, people talking in the background, or anything that will give the employer the impression that you are not a suitable candidate for the job.
3.) Make sure you follow up with contacts to whom you sent resumes. You don't want to lose the job to someone who is less qualified just because they are more persistent in their follow up.
4.) When you sent your e-mail, did you wow the reader with strong bullet points that will get their attention?
5.) Are you getting input from others? Ask at least three friends their opinions on your resume. A lot of people who spend time putting together their job search game plan neglect this important part of their campaign. Your friends' criticism is good because it will help you fine-tune your resume, cover letter and job search approach.

FOLLOW-UP SAMPLE LETTER:

Hello,

I would like to follow up on the status of my resume submission for the fore-cast analyst position, as there is a very strong match between the position requirements and my skills and experience. I've attached my cover letter and resume again for your convenience.

I have a strong desire to re-enter the consumer products industry and I would welcome the opportunity for an interview. With a track record of delivering up to $1 million in annual cost savings through accurate demand forecasts and supply-chain planning, I'm confident I could bring the same performance to ABC Co.

Sincerely,

Mike Mitchell

Functional Resumes

Many recruiters say that using a functional format instead of a chronological format is a good way to prevent you from getting hired. The functional format almost always raises red flags about your work experience. If you insist on using a functional format, be sure to include your responsibilities, the organization you worked for, the length of time, and useful facts that are of interest.

How a Human Resources Professional Views a Resume

Here's an HR pro's take on writing your resume: A resume should begin by telling the employer what they want to know. Each word should have meaning and allow the employer to get a glimpse of who you are and how capable you are of fulfilling the position. Many employers get tired of seeing the same old thing in every resume. That is why it is important to customize the resume to meet the requirements of the position for which you are applying.

Describe special projects, skills, leadership activities, or other useful infor-mation. Employers get numerous resumes and they are looking for some-thing that stands out. Your resume needs to tell the employer what you can do for them.

Some red-flag triggers for HR pros include gaps in employment, inconsistencies in work history, grammatical mistakes, and over-emphasized or fluffed responsibilities.

Lying or Providing Misleading Information

We all know the temptation to beef up your background by stretching the truth here and there to land that dream job. BEWARE! It's becoming more commonplace for companies to do extensive background and reference checks on a candidate prior to hiring. Also, companies that use staffing firms are demanding that their recruiters do more extensive background checks. The chances of being caught in a lie on your resume are forever increasing.

Recruiters say the most common resume fibs are:

- ✓ Inflated titles
- ✓ Inaccurate dates to cover up job-hopping or gaps of employment
- ✓ Partially finished degrees, inflated education or "purchased" degrees that don't mean anything
- ✓ Inflated salaries
- ✓ Inflated accomplishments
- ✓ Out and out lies about roles and duties

In the field of sales, for example, it's becoming common practice to subject applicants to personality tests, psychological tests, and aptitude tests. It's also common practice to do a thorough background check on the salesperson's personal W2 income and education. As temping as it is to embellish on your past experience, I highly advise against it.

22.) Resume-Distribution Services

There are several resume-distribution services on the web to consider. Generally speaking, they serve one or two purposes: to distribute your resume to thousands of recruiters and/or post it resume to a number of career websites. Here are the services offered by several career websites:

- ✓ Resume Zapper (www.resumezapper.com) will email your resume to more than 10,000 recruiters, including more than 1,000 recruiters who make international placements.

- ✓ Resume Rabbit (www.resumerabbit.com) lets you fill out one form that posts your resume on more than 100 career sites, like Monster, Career Builder and Hot Jobs (Yahoo).

Action Step: Research these and other resume-distribution services to see if they're a match for you. A few minutes here could save many hours of effort later.

Bear in mind that there are millions of recruiters and employers searching the internet every day for a suitable candidate who will become an integral part of their organization. This makes their work easier because they are able to select a candidate from the many databases across the internet.

These resume-distribution services allow you to choose the number of resumes you wish to distribute at any given time. Remember, the more resumes you send out, the greater your career options.

23.) Internet Career Job Sites

Web Career Job Boards

Indeed.com
Careerbuilder.com
Glassdoor.com
Dice.com
Simplyhired.com
Monster.com
Theladders.com
Beyond.com
Salary.com
Ziprecruiter.com

These are just some of the more popular career job sites for mainstream occupations. If you are in a niche occupation, you might want to find a website that posts job opportunities specific to your industry. A good way to find such career websites is to go through a search engine like Google, Bing, Yahoo, MSN, AOL. Use industry-specific keywords that relate to your job duties, occupation or industry. **TIP:** You can get more specific results on your search if you group the keywords in quotation marks. Example: Type "French chef" instead of simply French chef.

Posting Your Resume Online: Risks vs. Rewards

You can saturate the internet with your resume thanks to all these posting sites. But do you really want to?

There are three issues to consider when posting your resume online.

1. Placement: Where should you post it?
2. Privacy: How public do you want it to be?
3. Length of time: How long will it be posted?

You're probably thinking, "The more exposure I get, the better," right? Not necessarily. Recruiters get tired of coming across the same resumes in every database they search. If you get labeled a "resume spammer", you won't be considered for job openings they are working to fill. Also, the farther your resume spreads, the less control you have over it and the more likely it is to be discovered by someone you had hoped wouldn't see it, *like your current employer.* And yes, people do get fired like this.

Some of these problems can be avoided by limiting where you post your resume and by limiting the amount of information in your posted resume. It is possible for your resume to be visible but private online, but how visible you want it to be is up to you.

A few safety items of importance that you should consider when posting to a career website, or distributing your resume to thousands of recruiters, are:

1.) Read privacy policies – These usually tell you how your information is collected and handled. Some sites sell your information to third parties, while others are pretty good about keeping your information private.

2.) Limit the amount of information you offer on these websites – Many job seekers fill out a form with their contact information, then cut and paste the whole resume into the box, forgetting they still have their contact information in the body of the resume. It's up to you how much of this information you want to share.

3.) Limit where you post your resume – Post your resume only on a few of the more popular sites. This gives you maximum exposure for the geography, industry or type of company you selected.

4.) Don't let your resume sit and get stale – Renew your profile information every couple weeks so it's active and updated. Recruiters will look to see how long your resume has been sitting. But don't keep refreshing your resume on the same sites if you're not getting any job leads. If you are not getting any responses in a month or more, it's likely that the job or industry you are posting for is in short demand, and you may need to post your resume on an industry specific job board. Or perhaps this particular site is not effective for your search and you need to try another site.

5.) Modify the employment and contact information you put on your resume – If you have to create an e-mail address dedicated to your job search, check it constantly for responses. Try not to get too fancy with your job-hunt e-mail address. Keep it simple and not overly complex, and remember this is a representation of you. I've seen e-mail addresses that are surprisingly crude and unprofessional. Here are some acceptable, yet creative, examples: technolo-gyguru@aol.com, nurse911@hotmail.com.

6.) Delete your profile when your job search has ended – Leaving your re-sume on these sites long after you find a job can create problems if your cur-rent employer comes across your resume. Delete the profile as soon as you accept a position.

24.) Interviews & How to Hit a Home Run with Recruiters

A Job-Seekers Guide to Interviewing with Headhunters/Recruiters

You've probably heard of "headhunters", "recruiters", and "search firms" by now. If you are new to the job market or a veteran looking to make a move to a new organization, you should know the distinctions between these types of firms. Typically, they are third-party organizations that help individuals find temporary and permanent jobs. Here's how it's broken down:

- ✓ **Contract Recruiters:** Typically, an employer will hire recruiters from a contract staffing firm to represent them in the recruiting and employment function. The recruiters have an arrangement with the organization to "place" contract workers at the customer site for a period of time, sometimes ranging from as short as a few weeks to longer periods, in some cases a year or more. This might be important information for someone applying for a contract position at a company.

- ✓ **Employment Agencies:** Employment agencies work with companies that seek to hire professionals. The employment agencies submit resumes of qualified candidates to the companies, which interview the candidates and ultimately pay a fee to the employment agency if a selected candidate is "placed." In most cases, the placement fee is paid by the company working with the employment agency. In rare cases, the candidate pays a fee to the employment agency to be placed at an organization. If you come across a job listing that does not include the phrase "fee paid", be sure to ask who pays the fee before signing any papers. The types of positions that you might see a candidate paying a fee to an agency is retail sales, customer service representative, or a laborer position. These specific types of agencies can be found throughout the country.

- ✓ **Resume Referral Firms:** A resume referral firm collects information on job seekers and forwards it to prospective employers. This information can be contained in resumes or on paper or electronic data forms. The employer, job seeker, or both might pay fees. You must give the firm written permission to pass your resume on to employers. Your permission should include a statement that expressly states to whom and for what purpose the information can be used.

✓ **Search Firms:** A search firm contracts with employers to find and screen qualified applicants to fill a specific position. Search firm representatives will disclose to the candidate which employer they represent in the interview qualifying process. The fees for these firms are paid by the employer. The fee charged is either a flat fee equivalent to 20% to 30% of the candidate's first year salary, or an hourly fee paid to the search firm to locate a qualified candidate.

Questions to Ask a Recruiter

A recruiter may be helpful to you in your job search, but be a wise consumer. Read all materials carefully and ask questions.

Here are some general questions you may want to ask:

✓ **How many job openings are there for someone in my field?** If you have the opportunity, inquire about the positions being filled or the number of openings related to your field. These are important questions because, in some instances, recruiters may not really have the type or number of openings they advertise. They may be more interested in adding your name to their candidate pool as a means of attracting more employers or clients to their services. Or they may be collecting resumes for future job opportunities.

✓ **How is this information being used?** A third-party recruiter is allowed legally to share your resume with the contract employer for positions that you are actually seeking. The recruiter must tell you, in clear terms, that your materials and information will not be shared outside the organization or used for any purpose other than with the company they represent at the time they interview you. The third-party recruiter cannot sell your information to anyone else. You may choose to authorize the recruiter to share your data elsewhere, but your authorization should be given to the recruiter in writing.

✓ **Are candidates treated equally and fairly?** If you are qualified for the job opportunity, the third-party recruiter must pass your information to employers without regard to your race, color, national origin, religion, age, gender, sexual orientation, or disability.

✓ **Who pays the placement services fee?** Before you agree to anything or sign a contract, ask the recruiter who will pay the fee. He/she will normally tell you upfront who the fee is paid by, but you must ask anyway to be clear.

25.) Eight Steps to Success at Career Fairs

There are a variety of job fairs out there, and some of them are more worth your time than others. Some job fairs are specific to industry. Your alma mater might offer a job fair. There are also industry trade shows that have job boards or recruiting days, along with the opportunity to talk about jobs with exhibitors. You can find and research job fairs through local newspapers, cable TV stations, business publications, and college recruiting offices, but career fairs should only be a small part of your overall job search strategy. This will outline eight steps to help give you an advantage over the many other job seekers by making the most of your career-fair efforts.

1. **Register.** Pre-registering for the event is recommended, and most job fairs allow you to register online. You might be asked to submit a resume or summary resume. Pre-registration allows employers to prescreen applicants and make note of those they want to meet at the fair. Pre-registration does not guarantee that you will get noticed or that employers will even look at the registrations. Nevertheless, it's always a good idea to pre-register since it's easy to do and can reap big benefits.

2. **Research attending companies.** I cannot overemphasize the importance of going to the web and researching the companies with which you plan to speak. There will be hundreds, or in the case of larger job fairs, *thousands* of applicants who will be going to the same booth you plan to visit. Why will they consider you for their position instead the many others who have shown up and told them what a great candidate they are? When you go to a job fair, be ready to interview. Often the people at the booth are recruiters or human resource professionals. The interview begins as soon as you walk up to the booth. The recruiter will size you up by noting your attire, your demeanor, your handshake, and how you conduct yourself during this conversation.

3. **Bring resumes.** Bring lots of resumes to the fair, at least two for each company in which you have an interest. If you have multiple interests or job objectives, bring enough of each version of your resume. Make a good impression on recruiters by handing them a hard copy of your resume, collecting their business cards and promising to e-mail them a soft copy later in the day. Recruiters appreciate having a soft copy so they can reformat it when they present it to their clients or for internal use. Be productive at job fairs because they only last a day or two. Goal: Schedule an in-person interview with at least one exhibitor.

4. **Wear appropriate conference attire.** Conservative business attire is essential because image and first impressions are critical. Find out what is the expected attire for the conference and dress accordingly. It's always better to be overdressed than underdressed.

5. **Devise an overall strategy.** You need to devise a strategy or plan of attack for the fair. You've already done the first step by researching the companies you are interested in. The next step is to survey the layout of the fair and determine an order of interviewing. Some experts suggest meeting with your top choices first thing in the morning, interviewing with your other choices in the middle of the day, and returning to your top choices at the end of the day to thank them again for their time. But remember to stay flexible as your top choices may be the top choices of many.

6. **Hone your one-minute pitch.** You won't have much time to interview, so make every minute productive. You don't want to be screened out early. Develop a one-minute "marketing" power discussion highlighting the key benefits that you can offer the organization. Also remember the four keys to all interviews: Make eye contact, offer a firm handshake, show enthusiasm and smile. You should also be prepared to answer interview questions just as you would any employment interview. Conclude the discussion by asking, "What do I need to do to obtain a second interview with your firm?"

7. **Network.** Career fairs are all about networking. You're obviously building a network with the recruiters, but you can also network with your fellow job-seekers. Your peers can help by sharing information about job leads, companies, and their recruiting strategies and styles. There might also be professional organizations or employment agencies on hand at the fair, which are also good sources for networking.

8. **Follow up.** You would be surprised at how few job seekers actually take the time to follow up on their career fair interviews. Some experts suggest calling the recruiter the evening of the fair and leaving a voicemail message thanking them for their time. The more traditional approach is to write a thank-you note and mail it the next day. Thank the recruiter for their time, restate your interest in the position, reiterate your interest for a second interview and promise to follow up later with a phone call. Make sure you call! Enclose another copy of your resume with the thank-you letter.

26.) Aptitude & Career Testing

What are aptitude tests and how can they help you?

In short, aptitude tests are essentially skill tests. What they do is evaluate your ability to perform specific tasks. Aptitude tests help people figure out what your natural preferences are when it comes to working. Career assessment testing helps pinpoint your strengths and how to apply them professionally. Career tests can be a useful tool in narrowing down your best career choices. The objective of a career aptitude test is to help you understand you're natural or acquired abilities and how to identify the career choices that best match your aptitudes.

An Aptitude Test will measure your ability to perform tasks in these areas:

- ✓ Numerical Reasoning – your basic math test
- ✓ Verbal Reasoning – your basic understanding of the written word
- ✓ Spatial Ability – can you visualize in 3D
- ✓ Technical Ability – can you program your DVD player
- ✓ Acuity – the ability to do things quickly and accurately
- ✓ Perceptual Ability – seeing similarities in shapes and patterns
- ✓ Analytical Ability – solving word problems

One weakness I have found about aptitude tests is that they show your current capabilities, but they can't predict your future successes and how you will get there.

Helpful Tips on Psychometric Testing

What is a Psychometric test:

Psychometric tests are standardized, scientific tests – usually taken on a computer, which are used to assess your intelligence, abilities, potential and personality. Most employers who give these tests to potential employees as part of the recruiting process use them as a way to weed out candidates that may not fit a particular employer's profile.

Here are tips to ace a psychometric test:

- ✓ Arrive on time for the testing, but don't rush, it will take too long for your nerves to calm down. You should be relaxed, free of any distractions, and ready for the test.
- ✓ Ask the administrator if you do not understand the process at the instruction stage.
- ✓ Don't allow yourself to be distracted by other people. Concentrate on yourself and your own goal. Pay attention to the administrator.
- ✓ Stay relaxed. Don't get worked up or you will find concentration difficult. Though the questions in these tests are rarely complicated, you must relax to ensure that you provide correct answers. Panicking will make you lose focus and give answers that you would not give under normal conditions.
- ✓ Don't skip questions; answer all questions from beginning to end. If you genuinely can't answer a question, leave it until the end and go back to it if time permits. These questions may be simpler when you have completed the rest of the test. Good luck!

Personality Profiling

The aptitude test is only one part of the testing process; you must also complete a personality profile. A high score in an aptitude test is great, but it does not determine that you will be suited to the actual position you are seeking. Participating in a personality profile ensures that this mismatch doesn't happen.

A profile questionnaire measures the following personality traits:

- What type of work style do you have?
- How do you relate to other people?
- What motivates you?
- How do you deal with emotional situations?
- How do you react in a stressful situation?
- How do you deal with stress?
- Is your outlook on life positive or negative?

Don't second-guess the test. Remember, there are no right or wrong answers. The test will fail if you provide information that is contrary to what you believe. The tests have built-in checks to detect whether you are telling the truth. Testers won't look at the "accuracy" of your answers. Instead, they develop an overview of your characteristics based on your answers. Be true to yourself and answer each question honestly. This test gives an employer an insight into your decision-making capabilities and your sense of logic and balance.

Testing will vary from organization to organization, as tests are designed to meet the specific needs of the hiring company. Tests normally run from 30 minutes to as long as a couple hours, depending on position type and business needs.

You must score a minimum of 66% to pass these tests, so concentration is key. Overcome your nerves by reminding yourself that there are easy questions at the beginning of the test. Relax and answer each question to the best of your ability.

Career Testing: Assessing Your Numerical Reasoning Skills

Employers test your numerical reasoning skills to determine your knowledge and its application in the resolution of mathematical problems. Many of the questions are based on calculating ability and basic mathematics.

Many of the questions involved are looking to see how you identify patterns. You'll get a series of numbers and you will need to identify the sequence or relationship between the numbers. Here's an example:

3, 6, 9, 13

The number that doesn't fit is 13, because it is not a multiple of three and the others are sequential. Patterns and combinations questions are generally asked at the beginning of the test. It is an effective way to measure how you view things and if you are tuned into the overall picture. There will be a series of multiplication and division questions that may involve more complex numbers or equations. This is an attempt to see how you apply lateral thinking. Revert back to your basic mathematical principles and apply them as you answer all these numerical problems.

Career Testing: Assessing Your Problem-Solving Ability

Employers want to measure your ability to solve problems and identify solutions when faced with complexity. The purpose of the test is to identify your thought process and the steps you take in problem solving. You will be faced with some abstract problems and several different options as solutions. These tests are a little tricky, and there are pitfalls built into the test to check your approach.

Use the following tips:

- ✓ There is generally only one correct answer and very often, this can be the obvious answer.
- ✓ Read all possible answers thoroughly before you complete the question.

- ✓ Don't be misled by your instincts. There may be several answers that could apply but only one is correct.
- ✓ Look out for a pattern to the question, which will help you choose your answer.

Remember, employers are interested in how you reach a conclusion and how you face each problem. Take your time, read each question thoroughly, and review each answer before you proceed to the next question.

27.) Dealing with Extended Unemployment

We all know people who have lost their jobs due to downsizing or companies moving operations overseas. As the job market becomes more and more volatile, expect to hear more tales of unemployment. It's important to keep a positive attitude during this period, because when you go to interviews, your tone and mannerisms show through. You want to leave the interviewer with a good impression from the start of the interview until you shake hands and say goodbye.

If you are unemployed, you will probably do some thinking about your career. You'll reassess your personal and professional goals, ponder a career change and evaluate your job skills.

The first thing you should do is analyze the skills you used in your previous job, and decide whether employment in the same field is the best choice for you. If you're ready for a career change, look at your skill set and identify possible matches for a job in a new field.

When you sit down to write your resume, lay out a strategy and fine tune your resume. A few things to think about:

1. If the period of your unemployment was shorter than a year, don't use months in your job chronology.
2. Include any volunteer work you did as an intern, whether it was spending a few hours at the local recreation center or helping out at the soup kitchen. You should treat it like you would any other job description.
3. Don't misrepresent your employment status. If you aren't with a company, don't list your last job as lasting "to present". This can hurt your chances of getting the job because you were not honest about your current employment status.

Some employers are suspicious of functional resumes, because they are often used to hide gaps. If it serves you best, use a chronological format. This allows you to omit any short, temporary jobs if they're not relevant to what you want to do. If you are hired and required to fill out an employment history, you are obligated by law to include every job you've ever had. If you use a functional resume, be as specific as possible about the responsibilities that you've had as an employee and even as a volunteer.

In writing your cover letter, briefly mention your reason for returning to the workforce if you left voluntarily. If you were fired, don't mention it here, but be prepared to discuss the subject in your interview. If the job you're applying for now is significantly different from the one you left, you might want to explain what changed your mind about your career and what your expectations are of the new position. If you're returning to the same field, indicate how you've kept up with changes in the profession like attending seminars, conferences, workshops, and related college classes.

Laid off or fired

Losing a job causes more than a disruption in career plans. For those people whose work is a source of personal pride and value, the sudden loss can be disheartening. Some people understand why they were laid off or fired, while others are oblivious to those reasons. This is why you need to identify your outstanding accomplishments and how they can make a difference to a potential employer.

Remember to keep a positive attitude during this time. You will see the difference if you're upbeat and optimistic about your next interview and future employment prospects.

Prolonged job search

During an economic downturn, job searching gets tougher for those entering the job market for the first time, those looking to change jobs and those looking for work after being let go. This is where networking plays an important role in your job search. It's also important to identify usable skills and qualities and a proven history of adding value to a company.

Skills & Qualities

Everyone has some skills and qualities; some we don't even know we have. A way to harness these skills and qualities is to understand that you have them and to identify how to exploit them. Please see below some transferable skills and personal qualities.

Transferable Skills	Personal Qualities
Editing	Self-starter
Writing	Creative
Organization	Team Player
Team Leadership	Attentive to Detail
Networking	Excellent Communicator
Event Planning	Fast Learner
	Dependable

28.) *Interviews*

Job interviews can be tricky. There are companies looking to solve a problem by hiring a qualified candidate. But then there are companies looking to get insight or learn about specific products and services from candidates employed by the competition, just so they can get a pulse of what's going on in the industry. Ask questions during the interview process. You might be able to uncover why the interviewer has the opening and what their intentions are in interviewing for the position. Remember, the interviewer's objective is to find a qualified candidate. You'll give yourself a head start on getting hired if you show the interviewer that you understand and can solve their problem.

The only purpose of the first job interview is to get the second interview. Basic guidelines for the first interview include:

1.   **Punctuality** – Arrive early. The interviewer does not want to hear about the problems you had getting to the interview late. It leaves a bad impression.

2.   **Dress/Attire** – Dress to impress. There are two options here, depending on the position for which you are interviewing. You could dress conservatively, in dress slacks and business shirt, but for the majority of interviews, a 2-piece suit usually works well. If you choose the conservative mode, you will need to impress through conversation, demeanor, and your response to interview questions.

3.   **Listen Attentively** - Don't just *hear* what your interviewer is saying, but *listen* to what they are saying. Then, when the time arrives to answer questions, you'll understand the specific needs and objectives of the interviewer and the company.

Remember, it's in the second and subsequent interviews that you will attempt to "close" the sale. That's when questions will be more specific and you will have the opportunity to speak with numerous individuals within the company. You'll also be given the chance to ask your questions.

Essential to any successful job interview are the following characteristics:

Substitute strengths for weaknesses. Don't tell your interviewer you have no experience with a specific accounting software program. Instead, you could tell them that your experience with accounting software includes Quickbooks or Freshbooks, each of which you were easily able to learn quickly with some proficiency.

Attitude and demeanor matter as much as your response to questions. Be professional and focused, yet friendly and personable. Remember, you need to fit into the workplace. No one wants to hire an individual with no personality, no matter their qualifications.

Be brief, but thorough in your communication style. Long-winded, endless responses to questions are not the answer. You'll lose the interest of the interviewer and get "lost" in your own response.

Be enthusiastic. People love to hire individuals excited about their company. Be professional, yet demonstrate your interest and energy.

Demonstrate phone interview etiquette. Phone interviews for some job seekers can be terrifying. But you can develop techniques and skills that will maximize your phone interview's impact on the hiring manager. Here are some phone interviewing tips to get you going:

Pre-contact preparation. It's important to prepare for a successful phone contact when you are applying for a position. It's recommended that the last paragraph of every application letter include contact information so the recruiter needs to contact you with questions or request an interview. List correct working numbers where you can be reached. You should also mention whether or not it is acceptable to be contacted at your current position. Include your email address if you check it often. An applicant who cannot be contacted during work hours might include information such as "Although I prefer to receive messages at my home number, I check messages frequently throughout the day and can usually return calls during lunch or other breaks." Don't use music on your voicemail message, because this is very annoying to a recruiter and you want to impress upon them that you are a professional.

It helps recruiters if you leave one of these identifiers in the message: "You've reached Cindy, Jenny, and Tom. Please leave a message," or "You've reached 219-559-2113. Please leave a message." Again, each job seeker must determine what's comfortable. Don't change your message if you feel uncomfortable about having this information on your outgoing greeting.

If you have roommates, housemates, a spouse, or children, it's important to work out a system for message-taking. It wouldn't good if your toddler picks up the phone and says "Oh, daddy's in the bathroom," before hanging up. It might be a good idea to invest in individual voicemail boxes for each member of your household. Many new phone systems have this feature. In the event a recruiter's call is answered by a family member, instruct everyone – even youngsters – to carefully write down the entire message with contact names and phone numbers and remember to give it to you ASAP.

When you're waiting for a phone call from prospective employers is a good time to create a job log to have near the phone. My advice to job searchers is to make a list of the companies at which they've applied and the titles of the positions for which they've applied. Some people even list qualifications requested for each position. This way if you are called by the hiring staff, you will have some idea of which job they're calling about. Ideally, the interviewer would like to think his or her company is the only employer to which you've applied. But this hope dies quickly when you say something like, "Now what job is this again? I've applied for so many." At best it makes you look disorganized, and at worst, it looks like you're desperately sending out hundreds of resumes.

When you miss the call from the contact. If the hiring staff leaves a message for you, return the call as soon as you can. As you are returning the call, remember that the recruiter may have called 10 other people that day about the same or for a different position. Give your full first name and last name, say that you are returning the recruiter's call, and mention the position for which you are applying.

You're there when the contact calls. The moment of truth: The contact person calls and you answer. Here's how a typical call might begin: "Hi Adam, this is Jennifer calling from the Widget Company in San Antonio, Texas. I'm calling regarding the marketing analyst position. Do you have about 15-20 minutes so I can ask you some preliminary questions about your background?" Most interviewers like to make sure that interviewing now is convenient for the candidate. Most recruiting professionals will give candidates this courtesy, particularly when calling a candidate at her current place of employment or on their mobile phone.

A part of this preliminary questioning is to qualify your background. You should also expect questions about your work history, duties and responsibilities, length of employment, reasons for leaving current and past employers, compensation history and expectations, and maybe cultural questions about the type of work environment you worked in. The idea is to determine whether this position will be a good fit for you and the prospective employer.

When speaking to the recruiter over the phone, it's important to treat this phone interview the same as you would an in-person interview. Greet the person on the other end by saying good morning, afternoon, or evening, and say that it is a pleasure speaking to them and you appreciate their interest in you for the position. Remember to stay positive, and smile when answering questions or giving explanations. If the recruiter happens to call during a bad time for you, let them know right away and schedule the call for another time that is more convenient.

Here are a few things that you should always bear in mind: If you have a cordless phone, make sure the battery is fully charged. If you have kids in the house, find a room or space where you can speak in privacy without disturbances. If you live with roommates, make sure they don't have music or other distractions in the background. It's also important to keep a notepad handy. Better yet, have the notes from the advertisement for the position ready so you can speak intelligently about the position.

Speak clearly, take your time to answer questions, and ask questions about the duties and responsibilities for the position. Lastly, thank the caller for their time.

After the phone call. Write a short thank you note after the call. Here is one of many examples: "Thank you for taking time out of your schedule to talk to me about the marketing analyst position. I thoroughly enjoyed the conversation and have a better understanding of the job. I'd be interested in a second in-person interview to see if this position will be a good fit for both parties."

Online meeting services. Online meeting services are becoming increasingly popular among recruiters and hiring managers. The recruiter can send an invitation via e-mail to the candidate with specific login information to this service. The candidate opens his or her e-mail, clicks on the link and is directed to the online meeting service website to have the meeting. There are services that offer Voice over Internet Protocol (VoIP) calling, which allows you to speak to the interviewer through your internet connection on your computer. In similar services, you can also call into a conference number and log on to your computer to participate in voice and video meetings. The latter option is used more frequently by candidates who want to present their work through a PowerPoint presentation, Word document, or Excel spreadsheet. Some online services also request that candidates take aptitude tests and work- or industry-related skills tests.

More Tips for a Telephone Interview

✓ Do your homework and research the companies with which you will interview. The most efficient research tool is the internet. Visit the employer's home page, read articles written about the company, and go to forums that list the company with related articles about how they do business, etc.

✓ Keep a positive attitude a high level of energy throughout the phone interview. You don't want to put the person on the other end to sleep.

✓ Having notes with answers to certain questions should help you breeze through some of the recruiter's questions. When answering their questions, make sure you don't sound like you are reading from a script. It will sound obvious and they can pick up on things like that.

✓ Speak directly into the telephone and avoid using the speakerphone on your home phone or cell phone.

✓ Address the interviewer by their last name unless they say it is OK to call them by their first name.

✓ You should be focused on the interview. Don't eat or chew gum.

✓ Take notes. You should be able to learn the correct spelling of the interviewer's name and everything you wanted to know about the position by the end of the interview.

✓ Turn off call waiting on your phone (if you knew they were going to call).

✓ Give accurate and detailed contact information in your cover letter so your interviewers can easily connect with you.

✓ Don't get confused between the different jobs for which you've applied.

Phone Follow Up

If you were not told during the interview when a hiring decision will be made, follow up with a phone call and email 24 hours later, then another email two days after that. If they tell you upon your follow-up call that the decision has not been made, find out whether you are still under consideration for the job. Ask if there are any other questions the interviewer might have about your qualifications and offer to come in for another interview if necessary. Reiterate that you are still very interested in the job.

If you learn that you did not get the job, try to find out why. You may also inquire whether the interviewer can think of anyone else who might be able to use someone with your abilities, either in another department or at another company.

If you are offered the job, decide whether you want it. If you are not sure, thank the employer and ask for several days to think about it. Ask any other questions you might need answered to help you with the decision. If you know you want the job and have all the information you need, accept the job with thanks and get the details on when you start. Ask whether the employer will be sending a letter of confirmation, as it is best to have the offer in writing.

Legal and Illegal Pre-employment Questions

Pre-employment questions can cover a number of areas of your career and personal life. It's important to distinguish between legitimate questions and those that might be illegal and hurtful to your chances of getting the job. This is especially true if you have disabilities. You want to make sure that you are not discriminated against, so pay close attention to the questions and only answer the ones that are legal and give you the best shot at the job.

Illegal Questions	Legal Questions
What is your corrected vision? When did you lose your eyesight? How did you lose your eyesight?	Are you able to perform the essential functions of the job?
Please complete the following medical history as part of the application process. Have you had any recent or past illness or operations? If yes, list and give dates. What was the date of your last physical exam? What medications do you take?	As part of the company's hiring process, after a job offer has been made, you will be required to undergo a medical exam. The results will remain confidential and will only be used if emergency medical treatment is necessary or to assist in the determination of a job accommodation.
Do you have any disabilities? Do you have a disability that would prevent you from performing the essential functions of the job with or with an accommodation?	Will you need any accommodation to participate in the recruiting process?
Do you see a psychiatrist for stress or any mental problems?	How well can you handle stress?
Are you an alcoholic? How often do you drink alcoholic beverages?	Do you drink alcoholic beverages?
How often were you sick or take off for sick days?	What was your attendance record at your last employer?

	What are your job skills, educational background, and prior work experiences?
Do you use a wheelchair, and will we have to make any accommodations for the wheelchair?	
What is your sexual orientation? Gay or Straight?	
Do you have any kids, and do you plan on having any soon?	
What are your political affiliations?	
What is your religion or church? Will you require any time off for religious purposes?	
What is your nationality or race, and what is your skin color?	
How old are you?	

Now that you know what is permissible and what is discriminatory, consider how you might prepare for a situation in which the illegal questions come up. Your action depends on what makes you feel comfortable. There are three paths you can take for this type of questioning.

1.) You could forfeit your rights and answer the question, in the hopes that it will deepen your connection with the employer rather than incite bias. There might be times when you discover that your interviewer goes to the same church or has family from a country similar to yours. You might not hesitate to disclose this information about yourself in these cases.

2.) Alternatively, you could discreetly refuse to answer the question. For example, you might avoid answering the question directly but address the concern. If asked whether you plan to have children, you might reply: "I try to balance my work and my personal life. I can assure you that I will be focused and committed to my responsibilities here, and my personal life will not interfere with my performance." If you elect not to answer the question but you wish to secure the position, take steps to put the interviewer at ease.

3.) You might, after hearing some of the questions, have no desire to work for a company that probes into areas of your personal life. If you decide on the spot that you do not want the job, you can go so far as to excuse yourself from the interview and even file a complaint or lawsuit. If you decide to pursue formal recourse, contact the Equal Employment Opportunity Commission. Their website is www.eeoc.gov, or you can call them at: 1-800-669-4000.

Avoid Bad Interviewing Habits

Avoid bad habits and inappropriate body language in job interviews, such as:
- ✓ Chewing gum
- ✓ Twiddling thumbs
- ✓ Tapping a pencil or fork
- ✓ Using "um"
- ✓ Speaking too softly
- ✓ Fading out at the end of a response
- ✓ Humming
- ✓ Whistling
- ✓ Nose picking
- ✓ Touching your face or mouth, or scratching your head
- ✓ Sweating
- ✓ Smoking
- ✓ Stretching
- ✓ Touching things on the interviewer's desk
- ✓ Fidgeting
- ✓ Twirling in chair
- ✓ Staring
- ✓ Cleaning fingernails
- ✓ Using slang or profanity
- ✓ Calling the interviewer by his or her first name (unless asked to do so)

Handling Frequently Asked Interview Questions

Here is a list of commonly asked interview questions that you might get from your interviewer:

1. What are your expectations for this position?
2. Where do you want to be in five or ten years?
3. What attracted you to this position
4. What attracted you to our company?
5. What are your short- and long-term professional goals?
6. Why are you looking to leave your current job?

Be considerate and strike a delicate balance when responding to these kinds of questions:

1. It's not appropriate to mention personal or family topics, keep it professional.
2. Don't go off on a tangent about how you want to start your own business or run for office.

Typical responses to "what makes you the best candidate for the job" could be:

"I would like to let you know that I am the best candidate for the job."
"I'll make a significant advance in the organization within a short time."

Answers to other popular questions:

- ✓ *Would you rather work with information or with people?* Ideally, both. But the response should be tailored toward the job description and the relevant strengths in those areas.
- ✓ *What qualities do you feel a successful manager should have?* Here is where your mention of successful projects and resources managed will come in handy.
- ✓ *How would you describe your ideal job?* Your description of your ideal job should sound like the job you're interviewing for.
- ✓ *How much training do you think you'll need to become a productive employee?* Remember, the question is asking how productive you will be. Respond that you can be productive immediately. Answer with confidence, and make it clear that you have the ability to make an impact immediately.
- ✓ *Why isn't your GPA higher?* Don't make excuses. Turn a negative into a positive by mentioning that you were involved in extracurricular activities, which made you a well-rounded person.

Yes or No questions:

- ✓ Are you a goal-oriented person?
- ✓ Are you a team player?
- ✓ Are you willing to go the extra mile and work overtime?
- ✓ Do you handle pressure and stress well?
- ✓ Do you handle conflict well?

Never respond with just Yes or No:

- ✓ Always elaborate, and be prepared to give specific examples.
- ✓ Your examples should be current. Avoid using anything from high school or before that.

Questions that require knowledge of the company:

- ✓ Do you enjoy doing market research?
- ✓ How did you find out about us?
- ✓ Do you have any plans to further your education?
- ✓ Why do you want to work in this industry?
- ✓ What do you know about our company

Thought-provoking questions:

- ✓ Have you set goals for your career?
- ✓ What motivates you?
- ✓ What were your favorite classes? Why?
- ✓ Who were your favorite professors? Why?
- ✓ What did you like most about your school?

These types of questions require:

- ✓ Thoughtful responses
- ✓ Responses that are not self-serving
- ✓ Responses that are specific to the job

Money questions:

- ✓ How important is money to you?
- ✓ What are your salary expectations to accept a new position?
- ✓ Will you accept a counter offer if your current employer offers you more money?

Answering money questions:

- ✓ Find a balance. Money's important, but you should also consider things like total compensation packages with fringe benefits, extra perks and bonuses.
- ✓ Remember, job satisfaction in the total package is also important.
- ✓ Don't bring up student loans. The employer will base your pay on your worth to the company, not what your needs are.
- ✓ If at all possible, try to delay salary negotiations. We will talk more in depth about this in a later chapter. Don't give specifics until after an offer is made.

Asking for the job:

- ✓ Make sure you ask about the next step in the process. Before the interview is over, remember to ask for the job. If you don't ask for these details, they likely won't be volunteered.

Phases of the Interview

Job interviews are a two-way discussion between you and a prospective employer. The interviewer is attempting to determine whether you have what the company needs, and you are attempting to determine if you would accept the job if offered. Both of you will be trying to get as much information as possible in order to make those decisions.

The interview that you are most likely to face is a structured interview with a traditional format. It usually consists of three phases. The introductory phase covers the greeting, small talk, and an overview of which areas will be discussed during the interview. The middle phase is a question-and-answer period. The interviewer asks most of the questions, but you are given an opportunity to ask questions as well. The closing phase gives you an opportunity to ask any final questions you might have, cover any important points that haven't been discussed, and get information about the next step in the interview process.

Introductory Phase

This phase is very important. You want to make a good first impression and, if possible, get additional information you need about the job and the company.

- ✓ **Make a good first impression.** You only have a few seconds to create a positive first impression, and that impression can influence the rest of the interview and even determine whether you get the job. The interviewer's first impression of you is based mainly on your body language. The interviewer is assessing your overall appearance and demeanor. When greeting the interviewer, be certain your handshake is firm and make eye contact. Wait for the interviewer to signal you before you sit down. Once seated, find a comfortable position so that you don't appear tense. Lean forward slightly and maintain eye contact with the interviewer. This posture shows that you are interested in what is being said. Smile naturally and show that you are open and receptive by keeping your arms and legs uncrossed. Avoid keeping your briefcase or handbag on your lap. Try to appear relaxed and confident.

- ✓ **Use your knowledge of company information.** You should get this information about the company in advance. Be sure to prepare your questions in advance.

✓ **Ask questions.** Deciding exactly when to ask your questions can be tricky. Your chance to ask questions in the traditional interview is late in the interview. How can you get the information you need early in the process without making the interviewer feel that you are taking control? Timing is everything. You may have to make a decision based on intuition and your first impressions of the interviewer. Does the interviewer seem comfortable or nervous, soft spoken or forceful, formal or casual? These signals will help you to judge the best time to ask your questions. The sooner you ask the questions, the less likely you are to disrupt the interviewer's agenda. However, if you ask questions too early, the interviewer may feel you are trying to control the interview. Try asking questions right after the greeting and small talk. Since most interviewers like to set the tone of the interview and maintain initial control, always phrase your questions in a way that leaves control with the interviewer. Perhaps say, "Would you mind telling me a little more about the job so that I can focus on the information that would be most important to the company?" You may want to wait until the interviewer has given an overview of what will be discussed. This overview may answer some of your questions or may provide some details that you can use to ask additional questions.

Middle Phase

During this phase of the interview, you will be asked many questions about your work experience, skills, education, activities, and interests. This is the assessment part of the interview. The interviewer wants to know how you will perform the job in relation to the company objectives.

Your responses should be concise. Use specific examples to illustrate your point whenever possible. Although your responses should be well-phrased and effective, be sure they do not sound rehearsed. Remember that your responses must always be adapted to the present interview. Incorporate any information you obtained earlier in the interview with the responses you had prepared in advance and then answer in a way that is appropriate to the question.

Below are frequently asked questions and suggested responses. Give a specific example to illustrate your point for each question.

What is your weakest attribute? (A stress question)
- ✓ "I'm a stickler for punctuality and promptness."
- ✓ "I'm tenacious."
- ✓ "I'm a perfectionist."

What is your strongest attribute?

- ✓ "I am organized and manage my time well."
- ✓ "I work well under pressure."
- ✓ "I am motivated and eager to learn."

What do you hope to be doing five years from now?

- ✓ "I hope to still work here and have increased my level of responsibility based on my performance and abilities."

What do you know about our company? Why do you want to work here?

- ✓ "You are a leading provider of widgets on the West Coast."
- ✓ "Your company has a superior product/service."
- ✓ "Your company has the largest market share for your product in the world."
- ✓ "Your company is a leader in your field and growing."

It would help if you try to get the interviewer to give you additional information about the company by saying that you are very interested in learning more about the company objectives. This will help you to focus your response on relevant areas.

What is your greatest accomplishment?

- ✓ Give a specific illustration from your previous or current job where you saved the company money, helped increase profits, or improved processes.
- ✓ If you have just graduated from college, try to find some accomplishment from your school work, part-time jobs, or extra-curricular activities.

Why should we hire you? (A stress question)

- ✓ Highlight your background based on the company's current needs. Recap your qualifications keeping the interviewer's job description in mind.
- ✓ If you don't have much experience, talk about how your education and training prepared you for this job.

Some Questions You Should Ask

- ✓ "Could you give me a more detailed job description?"
- ✓ "What are the company's current challenges?"
- ✓ "Why is this position open?"
- ✓ "Are there opportunities for advancement?"
- ✓ "To whom would I report?"

Closing Phase

During the closing phase of an interview, you will probably be asked whether you have any other questions for the interviewer. Ask any relevant questions that have not yet been answered. Highlight any of your strengths that have not been discussed. If another interview is to be scheduled, get the necessary information. If this is the final interview, find out when a final decision will be made, and when you should follow up. Thank the interviewer for their time.

Do...

- ✓ Be attentive and polite when answering questions
- ✓ Answer questions clearly and concisely
- ✓ Ask relevant questions
- ✓ Be sincere and direct
- ✓ Use specific examples to illustrate points

Don't...

- ✓ Try to control the entire interview
- ✓ Be too serious in the interview
- ✓ Bring up salary, benefits, or working hours
- ✓ Take extensive notes
- ✓ Make negative comments about anyone or anything, including former employers
- ✓ Smoke or chew gum
- ✓ Look at your watch
- ✓ Let your depression or discouragement show

After the Interview

The interview process is not finished yet, so don't get overly excited. It is important to assess the interview after it has concluded.

After the interview, you should:

- ✓ Review what the job entails and make a note as to what the next step will be.
- ✓ Take note of your reactions as well as those of the interviewer following the interview. Include what went well and what didn't go so well.
- ✓ Assess what you learned from the experience and how you can improve your performance in future interviews.
- ✓ Send a thank-you letter shortly afterward, preferably within 24 hours.
- ✓ Thank-you letters should be handwritten if possible. If you don't have good handwriting, type it.

Standard Interview Questions

The famous "Tell me about yourself" question

This is something you should practice and perfect. It's the basic introduction of who you are and what you are looking for in a job. It will form the basis of your introductory message when networking, and your opening statement in telephone contacts with employers.

- ✓ Don't give your life story.
- ✓ Give a very brief overview which includes education, previous job titles, responsibilities and achievements. Target your response to the audience or contact with whom you are speaking, and the position for which you are applying.

What did you most enjoy about your last job?

- ✓ "I was able to set goals and find effective ways to achieve them."
- ✓ "I was able to use my analytical skills to implement corrective methods at a critical stage of the project."
- ✓ "I developed a new approach to process improvement which became a standard for the company."

How would your colleagues or supervisor describe you?

- ✓ "I have been described as a dependable worker."
- ✓ "I was able to take on a task through to completion with excellent results."
- ✓ "I have a knack for finding useful information about our customers' buying habits."

What can you offer us that other people cannot?

- ✓ "I have a track record of identifying little-known investments that produce a great yield."
- ✓ "I am familiar with legal loopholes and parameters that affect client's finances."
- ✓ "I am a certified professional with many years of experience finding unique ways to solve financial problems."
- ✓ "I require very little supervision and produce great results."

What about this job attracts you?

- ✓ "I am able to use my knowledge in market research to develop strategies that will give your company an advantage in the marketplace."
- ✓ "I share the same values as your company."
- ✓ "I am comfortable in a small business environment as in a large one."

How long do you see yourself with us?

- ✓ "I see myself here as long as I am making a valuable contribution to the company."

How would you describe an ideal working environment?

- ✓ "An environment that proactively looks at solving problems in a team approach".
- ✓ "A marketing support team that can assist the outside sales force with customer and product information that will help them close more business and lend help to customers when needed."

Controlling the Interview

Here are a few tips that should help you understand important details about the position, the responsibilities, advancement opportunities, workplace culture and company ideals.

1. Retain control throughout the interview. One way to do this is to start the interview by asking the interviewer what type of person will be good for this position.
2. Be proactive and ask questions about a typical profile for the position.
3. Establish a format in the beginning of the interview so it sets the tone for the direction you want it to go in the interview. If you start losing direction in the interview, you can get back on track for example by asking: "Could you please explain again the corporate culture and expectations for this position."

Job Interview and Damage Control

All interviews will not go perfectly, as much as we would like them to. This is why we need damage control. For example, let's say you arrive at the interview and draw a blank when the receptionist asks with whom you're meeting. It won't look good if the receptionist later tells the interviewer.

Here are some scenarios and fixes:

1. *Arriving late to the interview*. Call the interviewer or the assistant to let them know you are running late. If you will be more than 15 minutes late, ask if it is still OK to come in or if you need to reschedule. You can always use the traffic as an excuse. If it's an area you have never been in, say "I underestimated the traffic in this part of town," or that certain roads were closed due to an accident or there was a flood.

2. ***Can't remember the name of the person you are meeting***. There are a few things you can do to solve this problem. Call the operator at the company and ask for the correct spelling of the person's name. If you can't remember the first or last name, then ask the name of the person under the title the person holds.

3. ***Mispronouncing the name of the person you are meeting***. The trick above normally works pretty well. When you call the receptionist and ask for the spelling of the interviewer's name, also ask their pronunciation.

4. ***Spots or tears in your clothes***. If you have ugly spots or tears on your clothes, acknowledge it and get past it. Don't whine too badly, just move on with the interview.

5. ***Interviewer seems to have an attitude toward you***. Keep your cool, and don't say something you will regret. You never know who this person might know. Never burn bridges, even though you know you will not be getting the job. Show that you have class and professionalism.

6. ***You answer a question incorrectly***. This is a tricky one. You will need to be at your sharpest here, in case you answer a question incorrectly or did not understand the question. You can say, "Sorry, I spoke incorrectly," or, "Let me explain what I meant by that."

Success Factors for an Interview

- ✓ Do you "click" with the interviewer, was there chemistry and rapport?
- ✓ Oral and written communication skills
- ✓ Flexibility
- ✓ Confidence
- ✓ Self-motivation
- ✓ Leadership skills
- ✓ Interpersonal skills
- ✓ Teamwork
- ✓ Problem solving skills
- ✓ Proficient in a field of study
- ✓ Positive attitude toward work and co-workers

Establishing Rapport

Making a positive impression on the interviewer will go a long way, in some ways; it can help you get the job. So, connecting with the interviewer is important. This requires more than just smooth talking, dressing sharply, dropping names of high-profile contacts in the industry, or just plain being polite. It helps if your personalities click and you both have some common interests. But you don't need to rely on mutual interests to establish a good rapport with the interviewer. A way to generate good vibes is to listen attentively. However, this does not mean that you need to ask them about their personal likes and dislikes.

Use empathetic body language.

HANDSHAKE: Your handshake should be firm but not too aggressive. Extend your hand so it is perpendicular to the floor. If you extend your hand with your palm facing down, you indicate that you need to be in control. If you extend your hand with your palm facing up, you can appear overly docile. Try extending your hand with your palm relatively flat, so that you offer to make full contact with the other person's hand. If you cup your hand, you indicate that you distrust the other person.

POSTURE: Leaning back shows boredom or gives the impression of insolence. It is better to sit up straight and lean forward slightly, facing the interviewer directly. Crossing your arms in front of you may indicate that you are defensive. Try to keep your arms open, even if your legs are crossed.

EYE CONTACT: Eye contact is crucial. Look the person in the eye when you are speaking and listening. To avoid giving the interviewer the impression that you are bored, look away to the left or right.

Mirror the interviewer.

If you notice the interviewer is smiling, smile back. But if the interviewer smokes, don't light up. Mirroring works not only for behaviors, but also verbal statements. GIVE AN EXAMPLE. Again, this listening tool should be used with discretion. Too much can be awkward, so be alert and watch for your cue.

Ask clarifying questions.

If you do not fully understand a question, ask for clarification. Doing so signals to the interviewer that you are interested in what he or she is saying. These questions can be tricky, however. If you ask questions that seek clarification on issues that are tangential to the interviewer's communication, they derail the person's train of thought and cause people to become defensive or withdrawn. Yet asking questions that ask for repeat information will give the interviewer the impression that you are not paying attention. Before interrupting the interviewer to clarify a point, make sure that you are listening attentively. Follow the train of thought of the speaker, then pose a question.

Ask open-ended questions.

Open-ended questions allow the interviewer to respond as he or she desires, and also demonstrate that you are open to what the interviewer says. The responses might challenge your assumptions, so they mitigate miscommunication. They also allow you to steer the interview in a way that gives you information about the company and job. The information you gather from these questions will assist you in evaluating the company.

Types of Interviews

The Traditional Interview

In a traditional interview, you will be asked a series of questions which have pretty straightforward answers. For example: "What were major challenges you had and how did you find a solution for them," or "why are you looking to leave your current employer," or "tell me about yourself."

- ✓ If you are asked, "What are your career goals and future plans" the interviewer may want to know if your plans are consistent with those of their organization. You should let them know that you are an ambitious person and want to advance within their company.
- ✓ Another question that may be asked is "What are your salary expectations?" This is a delicate question and should be handle carefully. Always wait for the interviewer to ask this question, and if you have to give a number, give a range or say the salary is negotiable.

The Screening Interview

Companies use screening tools and techniques to ensure that candidates meet minimum qualification requirements. Computer software programs are often used to weed out unqualified candidates. Screening interviewers' goal is to determine whether there is anything that might disqualify you for the position. Screeners will dig for dirt and hone in on gaps in your employment history or pieces of information that look inconsistent. One of the things the screener will need to find out is whether you will be too expensive for the company.

Things to watch out for during a screening interview:

- ✓ Personality can go a long way, but it's not as important to the screener as verifying your qualifications. Answer their questions clearly and directly.
- ✓ Be tactful about addressing income requirements. Give a range, and try to avoid giving specifics. You don't want to lose your leverage this early in the interview process.

✓ If the interview is conducted by phone, it is helpful to have your resume and a few notes highlighting your strengths ready.

The Informational Interview

This is on the opposite end of the stress spectrum from the screening interview. Job seekers secure informational meetings in order to seek the advice of someone in their current or desired field and to gain further references to people who can lend insight. Employers that like to stay apprised of available talent even when they do not have current job openings are often open to informational interviews. These employers are especially likely to accept an informational interview with you if they like to share their knowledge, feel flattered by your interest, or thank the mutual friend that connected you to them. During an informational interview, the job seeker and employer exchange information and get to know one another better without reference to a specific job opening.

Informational interviews take off some of the performance pressure. The objective here it to gain valuable information, just as the employer is doing at their end.

✓ You should be able to pinpoint prospective employers. Through your interview you'll develop an understanding of what it's like to work for specific companies or individuals, and you'll be able to make informed decisions about what employer would be a good match for you.
✓ You will expand your list of contacts by collecting names from the employer with whom you interview.
✓ You will gather information from your interviewers that, during your later job interviews, will help you show prospective employers that you've done your homework.

The Meandering Style

This interview type, usually used by inexperienced interviewers, relies on you to lead the discussion. It might begin with a statement like "tell me about yourself," which is pretty typical, and can be used to your advantage. Interview styles such as these allow you to guide the discussion in a way that best serves your needs.

Here are some strategies which may prove helpful for any interview, particularly when interviewers use an indirect approach:

✓ Pay attention to the interviewer. Even if you feel like you can take the interview in any direction you wish, remain respectful of the interviewer's role. If he or she becomes more directive during the interview, acknowledge their move and adjust.
✓ Come to the interview prepared with highlights of your skills,

qualities and experiences. Do not rely on the interviewer to spark your memory. Jot down some notes that you can reference throughout the interview.
✓ Ask well-placed questions. Although the open format allows you to shape the interview, you don't want to run the risk of missing important information about the company and its core needs.

The Stress Interview

Employers view the stress interview as a legitimate way of determining a candidate's aptness for a position. A potential employer in this case might purposely have you wait in the lobby before the interviewer greets you. You might face long silences or cold stares. The interviewer might challenge your religious beliefs or your judgment. Be prepared because insults and miscommunication are common in this type of interview. All this is designed to see whether you can withstand the company culture, work environment, or other potential stress triggers.

Wearing a strong antiperspirant and remember these tips:

✓ Be prepared mentally and memorize your message before walking through the door.
✓ Even if the interviewer is rude, remain calm and tactful.
✓ Remember that this is a game. It is not personal.
✓ Go into the interview relaxed and rested. If you go into it feeling stressed, you will have a more difficult time keeping a cool perspective.

The Situational Interview

In this interview, situations are set up to simulate common problems you might encounter on the job. Your responses to these situations are measured against predetermined standards. This approach is often used as one part of a traditional interview rather than as an entire interview format.

The Behavioral Interview

Companies increasingly rely on behavioral interviews because they use your previous behavior to predict your future performance. In these interviews, employers use standardized methods to gather information relevant to your competency in a particular area or position. Depending on the responsibilities of the job and the working environment, you might be asked to describe a time that required problem-solving skills, leadership qualities, conflict resolution, multi-tasking, initiative, or stress management. You will be asked how you dealt with these situations. Your responses require not only reflection, but also organization.

Here's how to maximize your responses in the behavioral format:

- ✓ Any of the qualities and skills you have included in your resume are potential probing points for the interviewer.
- ✓ Anticipate the transferable skills and personal qualities that are required for the job.
- ✓ Keep in mind the situations you have been in, and identify the results of your actions. Present them in less than a couple minutes.
- ✓ Reflect on your own professional, volunteer, educational and personal experience to develop brief stories that highlight these skills and qualities in you. You should have stories for each of the competencies on your resume as well as those you anticipate the job requires.

The "Show Me" Interview

For some positions, such as engineers or trainers, companies want to see you in action before they make their decision. For this reason, they might take you through a simulation or brief exercise in order to evaluate your skills. This tilts the interview in your favor because it allows you to demonstrate your abilities through familiar challenges. The simulations and exercises should also give you a simplified sense of what the job would be like.

To maximize on this type of interview, remember to:

- ✓ Be professional and take responsibility for the task laid before you.
- ✓ Get a clear understanding of the instructions and expectations for the exercise. Communication is half the battle in real life, and you should demonstrate to the prospective employer that you make the effort to do things right the first time by minimizing confusion.
- ✓ Do some role playing and brush up on your skills before an interview if you think they might be tested.

The Directive Style

In this style of interview, the interviewer has a clear agenda. Interviewers ask each candidate the same series of questions so they can readily compare the results of their interviews. Directive interviewers rely upon their own questions and methods to entice you with questions and gather what they would like to know. This style does not necessarily mean that they have dominance issues, although you should keep an eye open for these if the interviewer should end up being your supervisor.

Remember:

- ✓ Follow the interviewer's lead.
- ✓ Maintain control of the interview. If the interviewer does not ask you

for information that you think is important to proving your superiority as a candidate, politely interject it.

The Group or "Tag Team" Interview

The group interview helps a company get a glimpse of how you interact with peers to let them know if you are timid or bossy, attentive or attention-seeking. Do others turn to you instinctively, or do you compete for authority? The interviewer also wants to know if you use argumentation or careful reasoning to gain support. The interviewer might call on you to discuss an issue with the other candidates, solve a problem collectively, or discuss your qualifications in front of the other candidates.

This environment might seem overwhelming at times, but here are a few tips that will help you interview successfully:

- ✓ Treat others with respect while exerting influence over others.
- ✓ Observe the dynamics and the interviewer's rules of the game. If you are unsure of what is expected from you, ask for clarification from the interviewer.
- ✓ Keep an eye on the interviewer throughout the process so that you do not miss important cues.
- ✓ Use this opportunity to gain as much information about the company as you can. Just as each interviewer has a different function in the company, they each have a unique perspective. When asking questions, be sensitive not to place anyone in a position that invites him to compromise confidentiality or loyalty.
- ✓ Treat each person as an important individual. Get each person's business card at the beginning of the meeting, if possible, and refer to each person by name. If there are several people in the room at once, you might want to jot down their names on a sheet of paper according to where each is sitting. Make eye contact with each person and speak directly to the person as you ask each question.

Multiple Interviews

This type of interview is commonly used with professional jobs. This approach involves a series of interviews in which you meet individually with various representatives of the organization. In the initial interview, the representative usually attempts to get basic information on your skills and abilities. In subsequent interviews, the focus is on how you would perform the job in relation to the company's goals and objectives. After the interviews are completed, the interviewers meet and discuss your qualifications for the job. A variation on this approach involves a series of interviews in which unsuitable candidates are screened out at each succeeding level. It's important to ask how many interviews are in the interview process, and who you would be interviewing with for each interviewer. For example, you might meet with someone in Human Resources, then a hiring manager, then team members you will be working with, and maybe even the president of the company, depending on the size of the company. I would be suspicious of any company calling you in for a fourth or fifth interview. In cases like these, they typically want to get industry or competitor information out of you. I would be suspicious if the interviewers are jotting down notes to competitor information, or how you do things at your current company. That should be a giveaway.

The Lunch/Dinner Interview

Interviewing over a meal can go one of two ways. It can be a catastrophe, or it can help you get the job. An example of a lunch gone bad is if the interviewer or candidate has an allergic reaction to the dish they eat. With some preparation and psychological readjustment, you can enjoy the process. Meals often have a way of getting people comfortable so they can facilitate deals.

Here are some basic social tips to help ease mixing food with business:

- ✓ If your interviewer wants to talk business, do so. If he or she and the other guests discuss their upcoming weekend plans or their families, do not launch into business just yet.
- ✓ Avoid foods that have been historically known to be messy, such as barbeque ribs and spaghetti.
- ✓ Take cues from your interviewer, remembering that you are the guest. Do not sit down until your host does. Order something slightly less extravagant than your interviewer. If he insists you try a particular dish, oblige him unless it conflicts with your diet or religious beliefs. Do not begin eating until he does. If he orders coffee and dessert, do not leave him eating alone.
- ✓ Practice eating and discussing something important simultaneously.
- ✓ Thank your interviewer for the meal.
- ✓ Who pays for the meal? Traditionally, the interviewer will pay for the meal.

The Follow-up Interview

There are a number of reasons why companies bring candidates back for second and sometimes third or fourth interviews. Sometimes they just want to confirm that you are the worker they first thought you to be. Sometimes they are having difficulty deciding between a short-list of candidates. Other times, the interviewer's supervisor or other decision makers in the company want to meet you before making a hiring decision. When meeting with the same person again, you do not need to be as assertive in communicating your skills. You can focus on building rapport, understanding where the company is going, and how your skills mesh with the company vision and culture.

Tips for managing second interviews:
- ✓ Elaborate on what you have to offer and your interest in the position.
- ✓ Be tactful with probing questions. You want to learn more about the internal company dynamics and culture.
- ✓ Be ready with a plan for negotiating a salary.

The Structured Interview

In a structured interview, the interviewer explores certain predetermined areas using questions which have been written in advance. The interviewer has a written description of the experience, skills and personality traits of an ideal candidate. Your experience and skills will be compared to specific job tasks. This type of interview is very common and most traditional interviews are based on this format.

The Unstructured Interview

Although the interviewer is given a written description of the ideal candidate, in the unstructured interview the interviewer is not given instructions on what specific areas to cover. There could be a broad range of questions to answer, so stay alert throughout this process.

Interviewing Strategies

The interview strategies discussed below can be used effectively in any type of interview you may encounter.

Before the Interview

Prepare in advance. The better prepared you are, the less anxious you will be and the greater your chances for success.

- ✓ Find someone to role play the interview with you. This person should be someone with whom you feel comfortable and with whom you can discuss your weaknesses freely. This person should be objective and knowledgeable, perhaps a business associate.
- ✓ Use a mirror or video camera when you role play to see what kind of image you project.
- ✓ Assess your interviewing skills. What are your strengths and weaknesses? Work on correcting your weaknesses, such as speaking rapidly, talking too loudly or softly, and nervous habits such as quivering hands or inappropriate facial expressions.

- ✓ Learn the questions that are commonly asked and prepare answers to them. Practice giving brief but thorough answers.
- ✓ Decide what questions you would like to ask, and practice politely interjecting them at different points in the interview.
- ✓ Evaluate your skills, abilities, and education as they relate to the type of job you are seeking.
- ✓ Practice tailoring your answers to show how you meet the company's needs.
- ✓ Assess your overall appearance. Find out what clothing is appropriate for your industry. Although some industries such as fashion and advertising are more stylish, acceptable attire for most industries is conservative.
- ✓ Have several sets of appropriate clothing available since you might have several interviews over a few days.
- ✓ Your clothes should be clean and pressed, and your shoes polished.
- ✓ Make sure your hair is neat, your nails clean, and that you are generally well groomed.
- ✓ Research the company. The more you know about the company and the job you are applying for, the better you will do in the interview. Get as much information as you can before the interview.
- ✓ Have extra copies of your resume available to take to the interview. The interviewer may ask you for extra copies.
- ✓ Make sure you bring along the same version of your resume that you originally sent the company. You can also refer to your resume to complete applications that ask for job history information (e.g., dates of employment, names of former employers and their telephone numbers, job responsibilities, and accomplishments).

Dress for Success

Tips for Men

Your appearance tells the employer how you see yourself. Your clothes, hairstyle and choice of accessories constitute your professional image.

- ✓ Shoes are very important. Make sure they are polished and appropriate for that environment.
- ✓ The best colors for men's suits are black, navy blue and dark gray.
- ✓ Depending on what type of interview it is, a pressed pair of dark casual pants and a dress shirt will make a nice presentation. If the interview is for a professional or management position, you may want to go with a suit and a pressed or laundered shirt. Although it is important not to over-dress, it is equally important not to be under-dressed for an interview.

✓ Select a simple tie. You don't want the interviewer's attention to be on your tie.

✓ It's always safe to choose a conservative color when it comes to your outfit. Safe colors include black, tan, brown, or gray.

✓ The sweater you select to accompany your suit should be white, off-white, beige, or a color which complements your suit.

✓ Choose wool fabrics in cooler months and linen in warmer months. Stay away from 100% polyester blends and stay in season with your fabrics.

✓ If the business environment is "casual" or "semi-casual", don't wear jeans, even if the staff does, and even if it is casual Friday.

✓ Carry a lightweight briefcase or binder briefcase, and remember to keep your binder closed so as not to show extra resumes or other important documents.

Tips for Women

✓ Don't wear excessive accessories.

✓ Don't wear excessive make-up.

✓ Shoes should be polished to a shine.

✓ The blouse you select to accompany your suit should be white, off-white, beige, or a color which complements your suit.

✓ A business suit is best in a dark color, with matching shoes.

✓ Your shoes should be comfortable and you should be able to walk in them easily.

✓ A tailored suit is always appropriate for an interview.

✓ Don't let your hair be distracting. If you have permed or curly hair, keep the look conservative and professional.

Tough Interview Questions and How to Overcome Them

The interviewer has a vested interest in protecting his company. Don't lose sight of why he or she asks the questions he asks. He or she will ask you questions to identify discrepancies in your employment history, red flags, or limitations in your skills or abilities to do the job. Let's say, for example, you took time off of work to open a business or took maternity leave to raise a child. That gap in employment on your resume might raise a red flag. Do you have a good reason for it? Do you know how to answer these types of questions? Questions such as these are difficult to answer, and many candidates respond by rambling on. Know how to respond to these critical questions.

There are three steps involved in answering typical interview questions:

1) Understand what the interviewer wants to find out. He or she

might have an agenda for the interview. They might be wondering if you are dependable, able to adapt, or a team player.

2) Don't give too much information. Saying less actually is better. Only answer questions you are asked. Present the answer in a way that is to your "best" advantage.

3) Take your time and respond to questions asked. If you know what they are looking for, you can respond by selling the skills and accomplishments that are relevant to the employee's concerns.

Here are some tough questions:
- ✓ Why are you looking for a new position?
- ✓ Your education does not match with the requirements of the position. Why did you apply for the position?
- ✓ What are your compensation expectations?
- ✓ What is your biggest weakness?
- ✓ Why were you fired from your last job?
- ✓ Why should I hire you?

It's important to know that some employers are more likely to hire someone who presents him or herself well, rather than a candidate with extensive credentials. The safest way to answer questions is to emphasize your strongest personal strengths, backing them up with examples that demonstrate your value to the company.

Research the Company before Your Interview

One thing you must do before a job interview is learn about the company and position. Here are some ideas to help you get started on this research.

- ✓ Gather information from the internet. Search the company's website and look through the web pages to find product information, newsworthy articles, case studies and company related information.
- ✓ Search online for forums about the company and what people are saying about the company.
- ✓ Contact the organization's public relations or marketing department and ask for the most recent annual report and other company literature.
- ✓ Read current periodicals and trade journals to learn about the latest trends in the industry. These can be found at your local library or bookstore.

For job descriptions, you can try looking in these publications:

- ✓ The Complete Guide for Occupational Exploration
- ✓ The Occupational Outlook Handbook
- ✓ Call or visit the human resources department and ask for a copy of their job descriptions. If you can't get it, you might ask competitors for similar job descriptions.
- ✓ The Dictionary of Occupational Titles

Important things to find out:

- ✓ What is their market share (if available), and how do they rank in the industry?
- ✓ Know what salary range is typical for this type of position. Learn about the company's competitors.
- ✓ Familiarize yourself with the employer's organizational structure. Read the company mission statement.
- ✓ Who are their clients or customers?
- ✓ Know the full names of the executive officers, including the president, CEO and CFO.
- ✓ Familiarize yourself with the company's products, services and brand names.
- ✓ Find out the locations of all operations, branches and divisions. In most cases, this could be found on the company website.

The manner in which you find information about a company will vary. The important thing is how you will use it and make the most of it for a great first impression in the interview.

Company Structure
Find out what the structure and scope of the company, and identify whether it is small, medium, or large. Is it a division of a larger company or owned by a parent or foreign company? Does it own other companies? Who are its strategic allies? Is it a local, national, or international company? Also discover whether the company has divisions and what they are. It is also useful to know at what stage of growth the company is. Have they recently grown or laid-off employees? At what rate? Using the internet, media, and personal sources, uncover as much as you can about the internal workings of the company.

Know the Customer
Moreover, it is useful to know how the company makes its money. Who are its clients or customers, and how many of them are there? Is it a family-owned business, or a start-up company funded by venture capital firms? Getting your hands on a shareholders report could be very helpful. This way you can

determine what the company's earnings or losses are. Compiling this information will enable you to assess the financial stability of the company.

Study the Market
You also must familiarize yourself with the company's market. What products do they sell, and who are their target customers? If they provide a service, to whom is it rendered? What is the nature of the products or services? These are the kinds of things you should be discussing when you sit down for an interview. In addition, it is also useful to know who the company's competitors are.

Employee Relations
Interviewing current or former employees will give you some insight as to how the company operates and how employees are treated. Are company earnings shared by employees? What are the salary ranges for various positions? Is there a benefits package offered by the company? Additionally, you should discover whether employees receive training or mentoring, how many hours a week the employees tend to work, and how long employees tend to stay at the company. Finally, you might check to see if any complaints have been filed against the company. This can be obtained through the local better business bureau and your state labor office.

Research the Company
I cannot overemphasize the importance of doing your homework on the company or organization you are interviewing with. You should have a list of questions, and be ready to ask them at the appropriate time.

Researching answers to interview questions is also important, and this will help you prepare for your interview. Doing this will increase your chances of getting a job offer, or an invitation to a second or third interview, whichever may be the case.

Questions regarding the position:

- ✓ Is this a replacement position or a newly formed position?
- ✓ How many people would I be working with?
- ✓ What are the hours for the position?
- ✓ How soon do you anticipate a decision being made?
- ✓ When do you hope to have the position filled?
- ✓ What is the accepted work attire? Business casual? Business formal?
- ✓ Who will be your direct report?
- ✓ How will your performance be measured?
- ✓ What opportunities are available for future advancement?
- ✓ What are the responsibilities and duties involved in the job?

✓ What type of benefits package is offered, and are they fully company paid or is some of the cost shared by the employee?
✓ Are you capable of performing the job?
✓ Do you have the relevant work experience?
✓ Do the organizations goals and culture match your requirements?
✓ Will the job challenge you?
✓ Can you see future progression in line with your career aspirations?
✓ Will the role motivate you?

Questions regarding the company:

✓ What is the company culture like?
✓ What are some basic goals and objectives of the company?
✓ Is the company growing or planning to open new offices, locations, or facilities?
✓ Is the department growing? Will there be new growth opportunities in the future?
✓ What products and services does the company sell?
✓ Is the company growing or downsizing?
✓ How does the company perform relative to its competitors?

Know Yourself

When the interviewer asks you what your short-term and long-term career plans are, what will you say? How about describing your ideal working environment? What are your strengths and weaknesses? How do you take criticism? How do you deal with conflict situations? What motivates you? What is your management style?

Get a head start on answering these questions through the following exercises:

✓ Make a list of three to five accomplishments that you enjoyed and in which you had great success.
✓ Describe three scenarios in which you felt highly motivated to accomplish something.
✓ Describe three scenarios in which you lacked motivation, but turned it into a positive.
✓ Think of two scenarios in which you were appreciated by your co-workers.
✓ Make a list of how your colleagues, staff, and supervisors describe you. Include both positive and negative feedback.
✓ Make a list of your best personal qualities and attributes.
✓ Think of a few decisions that you have made. Describe how you went about making those decisions and the outcomes.
✓ Describe conflict situations between you and someone else that were

both successful and unsuccessful. What were the results of both incidents?

Your Ideal Job

Describe your ideal job and boss

During an interview, a hiring manager wants to encourage open and honest communication. Employers want to delve beyond the candidate's basic skills shown in your resume. But you need some information, too. For example, what is an ideal candidate for the company culture? The idea here is to understand what is important in a position for the candidate.

Sample Interview Follow-Up Letter

Date - Month XX, 201X

Contact Name
Contact Title
Company Name
Address
City, State, zip

Dear Mr./Mrs._____:

Today's discussion was very informative, and I was pleased to hear that you are looking for a candidate with my qualifications and experience. I would like to express my interest in the position for which I interviewed. I am confident in my abilities to do this job, and feel my skills and background are a very good match for this position.

Thank you for your time and consideration. It was a pleasure meeting with you and discussing this position.

Should you have additional questions or would like to schedule another interview, please feel free to call me at (888) 333-2222. I look forward to moving on to the next step in the interview process.

Sincerely,

(Your signature here)

Full Name

29.) References

Personal and Professional References

Should you provide references on your resume?

References should be furnished only upon request. Check with your contacts, find out which ones to use as references, and what they will say about you. Instead of supplying references on your resume, use this space to add other important skills, work experience and to highlight your accomplishments.

Professional References

Include the following information when you provide a professional reference: reference's name, job title, company, address, phone number and (if acceptable to your reference) an e-mail address. Including a reference's job title can help promote your image if the person's title or position is similar to the job or industry you are pursuing. Employers are interested in feedback about you from someone in a related field or in a position of responsibility who can judge your work experience, professionalism and reliability. For example, if you are seeking a sales executive position, provide three professional references from a respected sales manager, a business owner, and your direct supervisor. These references build credibility for you as a professional and show you have contacts in the sales field. More than likely, you will be asked in what capacity you know the references, such as a former employer, co-worker, or business associate.

Personal References

When listing personal references, include your reference's name, job title, address (ask references if they prefer you to use their business or personal address) and phone number. If the personal reference is a co-worker, it can be beneficial to point this out.

Ask Permission to Use References

Prior to providing a reference list, ask each of your references for permission to use them as a reference. It's also to your benefit to let them know the types of positions you will be applying for and what skills are needed in those positions. Then ask them to discuss what they believe to be your best talents, traits, or skills when speaking with prospective employers that contact them.

Who are your best references?

The most important references are generally your superiors. If possible, include at least two previous employers as references. In contacting previous supervisors, potential employers are looking for information about the contribution you made to that firm. Subordinates and peers should emphasize your ability to be a team player. Clients should highlight your customer service skills and interpersonal communication skills. Most employers require at least three references. It would be good to provide four or five references. For example, include two previous supervisors, a subordinate, a peer or volunteer coordinator, and a client). If you have not had work experience, use professors as references.

What reference information should you provide?

Include all the information that a potential employer might wish to know. Include how long you have known this person, the best time to call, and their relationship to you (casual or professional). Some references prefer to be called at work, so give a work address and phone number unless they specifically wish to be contacted at home.

Where should you include these references?

Your references should not be part of your resume. Attach them as a separate sheet behind your resume, but only if employers ask.

Common questions that employers ask references

- What is your relationship to the applicant?
- How long have you known them?
- Would you hire them again?
- Was he or she usually punctual, or ever late to work?
- Describe how he or she works with other people.
- Tell me about his or her job performance.
- Is there anything else you could tell me that might give me a better feel for this person?

Do You Know What Your References Are Going to Say About You?

It's best to talk to your references before you send their names to a prospective employer. They will be more prepared to give an appropriate appraisal of your character if you have made them aware that they will be receiving a call

149

from an employer. It's also a good idea to furnish the references with a job description and specific background information that may be helpful for them to mention to the prospective employer.

Another option is to furnish the employer with a letter of recommendation. Some employers skip formal reference checking if they have a letter of recommendation in hand. If you are asked to provide reference letters, and if the references do not oppose, you can write the letters yourself and have the reference sign it. This way you have full control over what is said. Ensure that reference letters are current and written on the reference's letterhead.

Thank Your References

As a common courtesy, you should send your references a letter of thanks for taking time out of their busy schedules to help you. Also keep them posted on how things are progressing with your job search.

List and Prep your Business Contacts

Most people don't realize how many people they can use as references. It could be current or past co-workers, bosses or supervisors, clients, sales reps, business owners, or other professionals you regularly deal with. You would be surprised to know who will gladly say nice things about you in a reference call, and you might also be surprised to know who might not want to give a reference or give a negative one. The way to tell which will be the better reference to use, is to talk to your references in advance and find out what they will say about you.

When you call your contact, ask if they prefer to be contacted on their mobile phone, by personal or company e-mail. Make sure you get approval from your reference prior to them being contacted.

When you talk to your reference, outline a game plan of what you're trying to achieve and what you expect from them. It's important to emphasize confidentiality during these discussions. You might want to discuss how you met, and how long you've know each other, since these questions might come up. If the reference is close enough to you, you may also want to share the position you're applying for, and who will be calling them for the reference.

Do the Same for Personal Contacts

Employers check personal references to get a feeling for your character. Again, you can outline the same game plan when you contact them. Ask the same questions, like how long you have known each other, how you know them and what they are expected to say about you.

Keep In Touch With Your References

It's a good idea to always keep in touch with your references, and update them periodically. You never know who your references can put you in touch with. These extended networks could mean a job lead or interview. Send them a quick e-mail or give them a phone call to give them your updated information.

30.) Thank-You Letters

Thank-you letters express your appreciation after a meeting or interview. This also helps strengthen your position as a highly qualified candidate. Thank-you letters should also be sent to those individuals with whom you had informational interviews as part of your job search networking or research.

The thank-you letter is probably one of the most important but least frequently used tools in the job search process. Using this tool can set you apart from other candidates, so be sure you send a thank you letter within a day or two after every interview. Make it brief, warm and more personal than your cover letter, but maintain a professional, business-like style. In addition to expressing your appreciation for the interview and reaffirming your interest in the position, this is your opportunity to reemphasize your core strengths or mention some aspect of your background or experience that wasn't covered during the interview.

Here are a few examples of the types of thank you letters that can be sent:

Acceptance Letter. This conveys your decision to accept a job offer and confirms the terms of your employment. As a general rule, you will already have accepted the offer via personal meeting or telephone call, but don't forget to confirm your acceptance in writing. This is a good way to ensure that there are no misunderstandings before you actually begin your employment.

Declining Employment Letter. This is used to inform the employer that you are declining an employment offer or withdrawing your application from consideration. Select your words for the letter carefully so that it conveys your sincere appreciation and consideration of the offer; provide a brief explanation for your decision, but again, don't mention that you accepted a better job.

Thank-you Notes: More Than Just a Courtesy

In general, companies view a thank-you note after an interview as professional courtesy. In some organizations, interviewers get offended if a candidate does not send a note. With present-day technology options, it's easy to send an e-mail through your tablet or smartphone. We have found that a large majority of interviewers appreciated a note of thanks after an interview. Make the investment of a few minutes of your time to thank the interviewer and express your interest in moving the interview process to the next step.

In addition to showing appreciation for the time of the interviewer and establishing another point of contact, your thank-you letter should include a reaffirmation of your particular value to the company now that you have more information about the job. Use the note to market yourself to the interviewer. You can reference specific concerns and needs of the company as expressed by the interviewer, and that you were paying close attention to what was being said. Cite particular ways in which you can address the needs and concerns of the company and how well your skills match with the job requirements. Doing this fortifies the interviewer's understanding of your fit for the position, and it also demonstrates your interest in the position. You should take great care in drafting and customizing the note. For this reason, it is also helpful to comment on something specific that you appreciated about the interviewer or what he or she said. Make sure you keep the comments appropriate and professional.

If you forgot to mention something important during the interview, you think there might have been some miscommunication, or the interviewer expressed concern over some aspect of your qualifications, you can address these in the thank-you note. Your note communicates respect for the employer and reaffirms your case as a candidate, and it also provides you with a good excuse for calling the employer again to follow up.

Thank-you note reminders
- ✓ A note should be sent within 24 hours of the interview, either via USPS or by e-mail.
- ✓ Make the note personal, but professional.
- ✓ Keep the tone positive and confident.
- ✓ Make sure you send one note to each person with whom you interviewed.
- ✓ Refer to specific items or topics that the interviewer mentioned during the interview.
- ✓ Reaffirm the value you can bring to the company.
- ✓ Check for grammatical or spelling errors in the note.
- ✓ Keep the note brief. Use your words wisely.

Follow up on the thank-you letter with a phone call a week later if you have not yet heard from the employer.

Sample Thank-You Letters

Thank-you Letter after the Interview

(Current Date)

Robert Rhodes
555 West 23rd Street
Apt. 402
New York, NY 10010
(212) 987-1234

Mr. John Jones, Manager Sales & Marketing
XYZ Corporation
702 Park Ave.
New York, NY 10010

Dear Mr. Jones:

I would like to express my appreciation for the chance to meet with you regarding your opening for a marketing representative. From what I gathered in the interview, this sounds like an exciting and challenging opportunity, and I would like to express my interest in the position.

Of particularly interest to me was our discussion on the marketing plan for the next five years and the approach through which the company will execute this plan. It was clear to see that your company has done all the due diligence and research to make this plan a success. With a talented marketing representative, I feel that I would be able to achieve assigned quotas, leverage existing business relationships and develop new business. I was also pleased to hear that the marketing representative has an important role in this plan. I could be an instrumental part of this plan. As we discussed, I have consistently achieved my quotas for the past seven years and have established new business accounts in the healthcare industry. The experience and expertise gained from my past experience would be beneficial in meeting your needs.

Again, I am very interested in this position and believe that, with my overall qualifications and experience, I could make a significant contribution to the marketing team at XYZ Corporation. Thank you again for your time and I look forward to hearing from you soon.

Sincerely,

Robert Rhodes

<u>Conservative or Formal Sample Thank-you Letter</u>

(Current Date)

Robert Rhodes
555 West 23rd Street
Apt. 402
New York, NY 10010
(212) 987-1234

Mr. John Jones, Manager of Sales & Marketing
XYZ Corporation
702 Park Ave.
New York, NY 10010

Dear Mr. Jones:

I would like to thank you very much for interviewing me yesterday for the electrical engineer position. I enjoyed meeting you and learning about your organization, the responsibilities involved and what the expectations are for this position.

After our discussion, I found myself very interested in working for XYZ Corporation in this capacity. I strongly believe my work experience and historical accomplishments make me a good candidate for this position, and I'm certain I could make a significant contribution to the engineering team over time.

In closing, I would like to reiterate my sincere interest in the position and in working with you and your tem. Your organization provides the kind of opportunity I am seeking. Please feel free to call me at the number listed above if you have further questions.

Thanks again for the interview and for your consideration.

Sincerely,

Robert Rhodes

Creative or Informal Sample Thank-you Letter

(Current Date)

Dear Jennifer,

I want to thank you for interviewing me for the creative director position this week. It was a pleasure meeting you and discussing the position in detail. As you may have heard during the interview, I'm very enthusiastic about the possibility of joining your team. I'm confident my skills and experience would add to the excellent job your organization is already doing.

Thanks so much for the chance to discuss my background and qualifications.

Warmest Regards,

Amy Roberts

Letter of Withdrawal during the Job Search

(Current Date)

Robert Rhodes
555 West 23rd Street
Apt. 402
New York, NY 10010
(212) 987-1234

Mr. John Jones, Manager Sales & Marketing
XYZ Corporation
702 Park Ave.
New York, NY 10010

Dear Mr. Jones:

I am writing this letter with great regret to inform you that I am withdrawing my application for the marketing analyst position we discussed last week. As I indicated then, I have a strong interest in relocating to the Midwest and have been exploring several career opportunities in that area. Just a few days ago, I was offered and accepted a position with an advertising firm in Illinois.

I wish to express my sincere appreciation for your time and interest in my background during our interview. I truly enjoyed meeting you and learning more about XYZ Company and the exciting projects you have planned.

Again, thank you for your consideration.

Sincerely,

Robert Rhodes

Letter of Rejection after a Job Offer

(Current Date)

Robert Rhodes
555 West 23rd Street
Apt. 402
New York, NY 10010
(212) 987-1234

Mr. John Jones, Manager Sales & Marketing
XYZ Corporation
702 Park Ave.
New York, NY 10010

Dear Mr. Jones:

Thank you for offering me the medical assistant position with your organization. I appreciate your interest and confidence in my ability to handle the many challenges this position faces.

This position is indeed a challenging one which would make good use of someone's education and work experience, in addition to strengthen overall skills and qualifications. However, after careful consideration, I have decided to pursue other options which will more closely match my career goals.

Thanks again for your time and consideration. It was a pleasure meeting with you and learning about your organization.

Sincerely,

Robert Rhodes

Letter of Acceptance after a Job Offer

(Current Date)

Robert Rhodes
555 West 23rd Street
Apt. 402
New York, NY 10010
(212) 987-1234

Mr. John Jones, Manager Sales & Marketing
XYZ Corporation
702 Park Ave.
New York, NY 10010

Dear Mr. Jones:

Per our phone discussion yesterday, I am pleased to accept your employment offer for the computer software engineer position. The position is an excellent match with my skills and experience, and I am confident that I can make a significant contribution to your organization.

As we agreed, I will plan on starting work on Monday, March 1, at which time I will complete the necessary paperwork and attend your new employee orientation. I understand that the starting salary will be $5,000 per month.

I look forward to joining your organization and becoming part of your software development team. Thanks again for your time and assistance throughout the interview and selection process.

Sincerely,

Robert Rhodes

Sample Thank-you Note

Dear Mr. Jones,

Thank you for taking the time out of your schedule to interview me on Monday, Jan. 7. It was refreshing to hear that your firm is one of a few in the country that really cares about your customers and their needs. Your organization is one that is admired and revered throughout the medical industry, and I feel my contribution as a project manager would make this firm that much better. It makes me feel confident that I would fit into the culture at XYZ Corporation.

After our interview, I reflected on some of the skills and qualities you indicated are most important in this position: project management, market research, flexibility and the ability to establish strong relationships with clients. In my experience as a project manager, I have been responsible for managing teams of professionals, and implementing complicated content management systems in large organizations throughout North America. I am adept at building strong rapport with clients at the executive level, and identifying clear objectives and expectations. I can immediately add value to your development team.

In short, I am confident that the project manager position would be a good career move for me, and that I would be an asset to your team. I look forward to hearing from you.

Sincerely,

Robert Rhodes

Sample Letter
(Thank-you Letter After Interview)

I would like to express my appreciation for the chance to visit with you regarding your opening for a marketing analyst. After reviewing my notes from the interview, and looking over the job description again, it sounds like this is an exciting and challenging opportunity and I want to reaffirm my strong interest in the position.

I was particularly interested in our discussion of the market research surveys you are planning to develop over the next year. As we discussed, I recently completed a similar project where I designed a survey template that is now being used on a regular basis to measure spending habits of customers in the Atlanta, GA market. The experience and expertise gained from this assignment would be especially beneficial in developing an effective tool to meet your needs.

Letter Format Should You Accept the Position

Date

Candidate Name
Candidate Address

Contact Name
Contact Title
Company Name
Company Address

Dear Mr./Ms. Contact Last Name:

First Paragraph: Express your sincere appreciation for the job offer. Identify the position you are accepting.

Second Paragraph: Remember to cover the necessary details such as the agreed start date for employment, location, benefits, duties and responsibilities, expectations from job, and lastly starting salary.

Concluding Paragraph: Indicate your enthusiasm about beginning your new job. Reiterate your appreciation for the offer.

Sincerely,

Candidate Name

31.) Job Offers

Negotiating Terms

When there is a job offer on the table, it's time to negotiate a compensation package.

The company is investing time and resources in securing you as the candidate of choice. They have made this investment because they think you will be an important part of their team. The employer is willing to make this investment in you because they think you have the potential to become a great employee, or an employee that will be able to deliver on what you have promised during the interview process. The negotiation game is very tricky, so you need to go in knowing what questions to ask in order to put yourself in a good position during the discussion. Consider these guidelines for more effective negotiations.

Find out what you are worth. It's almost a guarantee that the representative negotiating the terms of employment on the company's behalf knows the market value for your skills and experience. When negotiations begin, you should also know how much your work is worth. Using a few sources including the internet, do research on the salary and compensation ranges for comparable jobs in your geographic area. When researching these sources, take into account the cost of living differences between cities, especially if you are considering a position out of state.

Set a clear goal and objective. Many people who negotiate salaries really don't have a game plan or even know how to execute it, and as a result most people are not getting what they are really worth. Those who set clear and aggressive goals achieve more favorable results than those who aim low or do not set goals at all. If you want $50,000 a year, shoot for $60,000 to $70,000 and you'll be in a stronger negotiating position.

Set a minimum acceptance price. You should know your own financial obligations and responsibilities prior to accepting a position. If you know that you cannot take anything under $55,000, it makes no sense to accept the position. You should be able to decline an offer if it doesn't meet your financial needs. You should also take into consideration other factors of the offer, like any alternative options prior to accepting the offered position. If you are currently making $45,000 a year and there are no other offers on the table, settling at the same amount or just a slightly higher amount might not be a bad idea.

Strike a fair balance. Obtaining a compensation package that both you and the employer consider fair is particularly important since you are entering into an ongoing working relationship. If three months into your new job you discover that you are making 25% less than your counterparts, your enthusiasm for your new job can quickly diminish. On the other hand, if your employer feels like you bullied him into a costlier package than the company authorized him to offer, he or she could easily become resentful toward you.

Are you worth more than most people because you have more experience or because you have a long track record of attracting large clients or managing large projects? You must be able to make a strong business case for why your self-serving version of fairness is appropriate. Perhaps the rationale for your standard of fairness has little to do with you personally, and everything to do with asking for the market value of your work. Maybe you are asking for a salary that is commensurate with others performing the same role in the company or in the industry. It is helpful for you to identify what your employer considers fair, because you and your potential employer might be far off on a potential salary number. Remember: If your negotiating counterpart makes concessions, they need to be able to justify their concessions to their boss.

Identify all your interests. Both you and your employer probably have concerns or aspirations that are not strictly monetary. You might want to negotiate one or more flex days per week, for example, or have the ability to work from home a few times a month if you have to pick up or drop your children from school.

When you walk into the negotiation, prioritize your interests and identify areas where you are willing to trade one thing of value for something else. Is the salary more important than stock options? Is a health club membership more important than a likely promotion in six to twelve months?

Negotiating terms of the deal are very important. Discovering what your employer's interests are will benefit you.

Maybe the employer has some budgetary constraints and cannot go to the number you initially asked for. It's good to know if the negotiator has full decision-making capability or if they are representing someone else who makes the compensation decisions. It's likely that the potential employer may be able to offset a concession on your part by paying for your education, association fees, stock options, membership fees, or if the negotiation goes well, maybe a signing bonus. Remember to be creative and keep all of your options open.

Be competitive but allow room for negotiation. It's possible that the negotiator will be aggressive, brisk or stubborn, but keep your cool and stick to your game plan. If you encounter a negotiator who wants to play hardball, respond strategically. Don't allow yourself to get baited. Remember your goals, and why your requests are fair. Only volunteer information that will strengthen your position. If your counterpart makes a concession, it is important that you also appear cooperative. You might need to make a concession as well.

Letter Format Should You Delay Your Decision

Date

Candidate Name
Candidate Address

Contact Name
Contact Title
Company Name
Company Address

Dear Mr./Ms. Contact Last Name:
First Paragraph: Express your sincere appreciation for the job offer. Identify the position you are considering. Ask what the timeline will be for a potential start date.
Second Paragraph: Cover details of the offer you are considering, for example the position job duties and responsibilities, location, dress code, start date for employment, and agreed starting salary.
Concluding Paragraph: Reiterate your appreciation for the offer. Clarify once again the starting time period, and a recap of what was discussed and agreed. It is important to include contact numbers with instructions as to where and how you may be contacted in the interim. Thank the employer for their consideration and their interest in your background/experience and your request for additional time.

Sincerely,

Candidate Name

<u>Sample Acceptance Letter</u>

Mr. John Doe, Marketing Manager
Media Advertising, Inc.
123 Main Street
New York, New York 10101

November 1, 2005

Dear Mr. Doe:

It was a pleasure meeting with you on Thursday afternoon. I am pleased to inform you that I will be accepting your offer of employment with Media Advertising, Inc. I have spent some time reviewing this decision, and I am confident that I have made the right one.

As I mentioned in our conversation, I am obligated to give my current employer a two week notice. I will be able to join Media Advertising on or after Nov. 21. I look forward to joining the Media Advertising team soon.

If there are any other pre-employment details that I need to arrange at this time, please let me know and I will take care of them immediately. Thanks again for your interest.

Sincerely,

Robert Rhodes
31220 Warden Drive
White Plains, NY 10101
Ph: 708-444-0909
E-mail: rroberts@mail.com

Evaluating a Job Offer

Upon receiving a job offer, you are faced with a difficult decision and must evaluate the offer carefully. Most companies will not expect you to accept or reject an offer immediately. When evaluating a job offer, there are many things you will be asking yourself. Will the job be interesting? Will the company be a good place to work? Are there opportunities for advancement? Are the benefits any good? Is the salary fair?

Background on the Organization

Here is a step where due diligence should be done. Get as much background information about the organization to help you to decide whether it is a good place for you to work. Important factors to consider are the organization's type of business, its financial condition, size of the company, how long it's been around, its location and its company culture. Most of this information can be obtained through the internet, calling the receptionist of this company and asking for a company brochure and an annual report, or telephoning its public relations office. An annual report should give you useful information about the company's products, services, goals and financial status. You might want to ask at the company if they have a company newsletter, recruitment brochure or press releases you can view.

There are also additional sources that you can get company information:

Additional information like reference directories about the organization may be available at your public library, college/university or local school library. Reference directories provide basic facts about the company, such as earnings, products and services, and number of employees.

Some directories widely available in libraries include:

- ✓ *Dun & Bradstreet's Corporate Directory (online and hard copies available)*
- ✓ *Moody's Industrial Manual*
- ✓ *Ward's Business Directory*
- ✓ *Thomas' Register of American Manufacturers*
- ✓ *Standard and Poor's Register of Corporations*

A few questions you should ask yourself when evaluating a job offer:

What is the size of the company, and will the size of the organization affect you?

Most large organizations generally offer a greater variety of training programs,

167

better benefits and more managerial level advancement opportunities. Larger firms typically have more advanced technologies, and smaller firms offer broader authority and responsibility.

Would working for a start-up or an established company be a better choice?

New businesses have a high failure rate, but for many people, the excitement of helping build a smaller company has rewards if the business is successful. But if the company does not get off the ground you run the risk of job loss.

Does it make a difference to you if the company is private or publicly held?

Private and public companies have distinct differences in how they are structured. An individual or a family may control a privately owned company with family members in key positions. A board of directors responsible to the stockholders controls a publicly owned company and these key jobs are usually open to shareholders.

Is this organization in an industry that has long-term growth or many potential prospects?

Successful firms tend to be in industries that experience rapid growth. One way to find out if a company is in a growth industry is to look at the business directories listed above, plus government labor studies. You can also contact local staffing firms to get an idea of current and upcoming trends and market movement.

What is the nature of the job?

It's a good idea to find out what the day-to-day work will be like. Determining in advance whether you will like the work might be a little difficult. However, the more you find out about the job before accepting or rejecting the offer, the more likely you are to make the right choice.

Where is the job located?

If the job is in another area of the country, you need to consider the cost of living, the time and expense of commuting, the availability of housing and transportation, and the quality of education in that area of the country.

How important is your job in this company?

An explanation of where you fit in the organization and how you are expected to contribute to its overall success and objectives should give you an idea of the job's importance.

Are the hours of operations acceptable for you?

With most jobs, a typical work week means eight hours a day Monday through

Friday for a total of 40 hours a week. Other jobs require late afternoon, evenings, weekends, or even holiday work. Some jobs routinely require overtime to meet deadlines or production goals based on customer demand. Based on the hours, you should consider the effect that work hours will have on your personal life.

How long do most people stay with this company?

After interviewing thousands of people over the past twenty years, I have found that the work force of the 21st century differs greatly from the workforce of 20 or 30 years ago. There seems to be a high value placed on jobs in the current age, but very little loyalty to any employer. It has a lot to do with how cultures have developed in the workplace over the past 20+ years. High turnover at your potential employer can reveal dissatisfaction with the nature of the work or something else about the job.

Does the company have a training program or an accelerated management program for future advancement?

Many larger companies offer continuous improvement and professional development training programs that are offered to employees to encourage professional growth and learning. Some smaller firms that emphasize professional development also offer such programs. There are also companies that reimburse employees for joining industry associations and user groups that help foster learning and networking.

What opportunities are offered by employers?

Good job offers allow you to learn new skills, increase your earnings, and rise to positions of greater authority and responsibility within the company. The company should have a training plan for you. What valuable new skills does the company plan to teach you? The employer should give you some idea of promotion possibilities within the organization. What can you expect on your path to career growth and success? If you are waiting for a job to become vacant before you can be promoted, how long does this usually take? When do opportunities for advancement arise, and will you be competing with other applicants from outside the company?

32.) Salary Requests and Negotiations

Negotiating Your Compensation Package

Rule #1 in salary negotiations: Do not discuss your specific compensation package with the employer until you have been offered the job, and one in which you should seriously consider.

During salary negotiations, you are not only talking about your monetary salary, but your entire compensation package. This includes vacation time, personal sick leave, health insurance, tuition reimbursement, and 401K.

Your base salary and performance-based raises are probably the most negotiable parts of your compensation package. Many companies allow you to select from a number of benefit options based on a total monetary cost. In other words, the company will spend a certain amount of money on each employee for benefits, and employees have some flexibility when choosing benefit options that are best suited for them. For example, employees with children might consider child-care reimbursement benefits, while other employees interested in going back to school might choose tuition reimbursement. Before you begin negotiating your compensation, decide which benefits are most important to you. When you are dealing with a compensation package, consider all the benefits the company has to offer, not just the salary.

The Salary Game: What Are You Worth?

As you prepare yourself to go into the second interview, chances are you will probably be discussing salary. Most people seeking a job get uncomfortable when it comes to talking about money. The bottom line is most people want to make sure they get a fair salary.

There are many cases where people start working without ever knowing what they will be paid because they feel a job is better than not having one. Often people fear discussing a salary because they are afraid the employer will withdraw the offer of employment. Knowing ahead of time what the compensation arrangements are eliminates problems later.

The employer will likely try to offer you a lower salary to start and promise to increase your pay based on your performance, or based on the company's profit. If an employer asks you about your salary, the safest way to respond is to tell them it is "negotiable." The first step in negotiating salaries is to do some research. Check the list of sources we mentioned earlier of where to find salary information, so you can research how much other companies are paying for the same position that you will be doing.

Remember to keep your cool during the interview process. You should be willing to negotiate, but don't be overly confident while discussing money, because it may backfire on you and you may potentially lose the position.

These steps are important in negotiating your salary. Being too demanding in these negotiations may put you in a weaker position for getting the salary you want. Employers are willing to discuss salary if they believe you are the right candidate who is worth the investment for the company.

Salary Negotiations

As with any other part of the job search process, the key to salary negotiations is preparation. It is very important for you to do your research before you begin. In order to determine the salary you are willing to accept, investigate the salary range that someone with your skills and experience can expect to receive.

How do you find salary information?

- **The internet** – You can easily spend hours searching, but be advised that you'll likely come up with a few good sources that require you to pay a fee for the service.
- **The library** – Your local library should have a number of references to use to find out the salary ranges for the occupation you are considering. The reference librarian can provide assistance in locating salary information resources.
- **(NACE) National Association of Colleges & Employers** – This organization gives salary survey snapshots of pay scales for a number of occupations.
- **U.S. Department of Labor's Bureau of Labor Statistics** – This is a good source of salary information for a variety of jobs.
- **Occupational Outlook Handbook** – This handbook is published by the Department of Labor and provides profiles for a variety of occupations. It gives insight on a wide range of general careers, hiring trends, jobs outlook, job requirements and expected salaries.

- **Job search centers** – These can be found in schools, libraries, community centers, or as part of federal, state, or local government programs. Such centers frequently keep salary information.
- **Your past experience** – Think about your past salary. Your previous salary is a starting point for salary negotiation if the positions you are applying for do not dramatically differ from your former position.
- **Professional associations** – These associations conduct salary surveys both nationally and regionally. They provide salary and compensation information received from their membership.
- **Your network** – Talk to colleagues in your professional network about salary ranges and benefits.
- **Salary.com** – This is also a good source for salary comparison in your market and geography. This should be a good benchmark you can work from.

What about salaries and benefits? Wait for the employer to introduce these subjects. Some companies will not talk about pay until they have decided to hire you. In order to know if their offer is reasonable, you need to find out what a rough estimate is of what the job should pay. Try talking to family, friends, or acquaintances who were recently hired in similar jobs. You can look at help-wanted ads in newspapers, internet career websites and even do looks-ups on search engines. We will talk more about these sources in the following chapter. At the time of the offer, you must understand exactly what benefits are offered, what they cover, what deductibles (if any) apply, and whether there are any co-pays for office visits, emergency visits and prescription drugs.

It's important to learn the organization's policy regarding overtime. Depending on the job duties, you might or might not be exempt from laws requiring the employer to compensate you for overtime. Find out how many hours you will be expected to work each week and whether you will receive overtime pay or compensatory time off for working more than the specified number of hours in a week.

Take into account that your starting salary is just that, a starting compensation. Your salary should be reviewed on a regular basis. Depending on the role or position you are in, it may be reviewed quarterly, semi-annually, or annually. How much can you expect to earn after one, two, three or more years? It is hard for employers to gauge pay increases like commissions and bonuses over a period of time, because they have to consider many factors like the state of the economy, years of service, and most importantly your performance. If you do not expect to get commissions or bonuses, a general rule of thumb is that if you are entitled to a pay increase. Raises of 5% to 10% of your annual salary or compensation is common.

The Negotiation Meeting

Once you get an idea for the type of salary and benefits you are willing to accept, it's time to negotiate with the company. Don't sell yourself short during these negotiations. Usually, when a company is ready to make you an offer, they have invested a lot of time and money in their search for a qualified employee. You don't want to be too aggressive with the employer, but you do want to receive a fair compensation package. If the employer makes you an offer that does not seem acceptable, discuss your concerns with the employer. It's important to present your concerns about the compensation and benefits package in a constructive, non-threatening manner. Address the reasons for your concerns. Avoid making general statements about what you think you deserve or what you are worth.

When you are considering an offer, consider the entire benefits package. Sometimes excellent benefits can compensate for a lower-than-expected salary. If you really want the job, but the offer still seems low after negotiations, ask the employer if they will consider a salary review after a short period, say, three to six months from your starting date. Usually, you don't have to make a decision on the offer immediately. When you are presented with an offer, ask the employer for a couple of days so you can review the entire compensation and benefits package.

If you decide the offer isn't adequate, it's not advisable to state, "I must have more money." It would sound better if you explain that you would be making less than what you were currently making, and that you would like them to at least match the previous salary amount. If an employer is genuinely interested in you, in many cases they have some flexibility and can make exceptions for an applicant. They might not come back with more money, but they might come back with additional benefits (e.g., more vacation days or personal leave). In some cases, companies can offer a signing bonus to compensate for weaker areas of the compensation package.

If you get to a point where all the details are covered with the employer, find out when you can expect to receive an official offer letter in writing. It is very important to get the official offer documented. This means that management has approved it and the offer is genuine and legitimate.

Tips for Negotiating Job Salaries

Be prepared for the dreaded salary question: "How much?" By following these tips, you'll be more confident to handle this important part of the interview.

1. If the questions comes up about how much money you would like to make, avoid giving a direct answer. Give a vague answer, or perhaps give a dollar range until you have narrowed down what they are willing to offer.

How to Get the Best Salary Package

This process starts before you are even offered the job, and there are five steps that are usually taken:

1.   Understand your roles and responsibilities for the position before you agree to go to the salary negotiation phase.

2.   Negotiate the position.

3.   Show the employer that you are the best candidate for the position, and surpass your opposition. The company must need you and know the value that you can add to their organization before you discuss compensation.

4.   Get the job offer.

5.   Negotiate the total compensation package.

During the interview process, you will probably meet with a few people in the company. Among the first will probably be someone from the human resources department. As the interview progresses, you will likely meet with managers in the department for which you will be working. The important thing to understand is that you must influence all the individuals in the interview process, including the people in the human resources department. You have to convince the rest of the team that they need you and that you will be a perfect fit for their organization.

Many job seekers go to a job interview and accept the position without even discussing salary options. Most of these job seekers believe the salary the company offers is something you either take or leave. Remember that the company is already interested in you, otherwise they wouldn't have brought you into interview.

Be cautious in the interview process. Many employers will try to find out what salary you are willing to accept or get you to accept a lower salary. One method is to offer you the job and ask when you can start, with no mention of salary. Another is to ask what salary you need. Don't fall into the trap of answering. In order to get around this, explain that you really need to understand more about the position, the responsibilities and duties, the level of authority, and the accountability before you discuss any salary expectations.

As mentioned earlier in this chapter, company benefits, commissions, and bonuses are part of the salary negotiation as well. Remember, compensation is more than just money. You should also ask about vacation time, personal time, health plans and deductibles, a company vehicle (if applicable), expenses, flex-time, tuition reimbursement and professional training.

The counter offer: Here's where you will play hardball with the employer. If they offer you a salary that is not exactly what you were expecting, state what you feel you are worth and have your detailed reasons ready during this discussion. Let them make a counter offer. This is an important opportunity for you to show your worth and how you will contribute to the company's bottom line and long-term goals. You should also ask yourself why you want to be part of the company. Reiterate your relevant skills, accomplishments, qualifications and value added career achievements.

When you are presented with an offer, don't just accept it. Many people don't do their due diligence and review all the aspects of an offer. I cannot over emphasize how important this part of the process is. Ask for a few days to decide if this is really the job and compensation package for you. Does this fit with your long-term career plan? If this is not what you want and you believe it will not satisfy you, let them know right away. Remember you are in control of your career destiny.

If you like what you see in the company, and an acceptable offer is made, make sure you get it in WRITING! Everything that was discussed in subsequent interviews should be included in the offer letter, such as health plans, commissions and bonuses, vacations, and salary. If the company does not provide this in writing, I would certainly be skeptical and would likely move on to the next opportunity.

33.) Salary Information: What You Should Know

You are at the final phase of the interviewing process, and it's imperative to gather information prior to your meetings. In order to accurately assess your position, you need to understand your strengths, accomplishments, and available resources. The information that you gather will give you bargaining strength.

Important factors to help you capitalize on salary negotiations:

Know the industry:

- ✓ Do research on what the demand is for the industry in which you are employed.
- ✓ Understand the status of the economy and how it affects the industry you are competing in.
- ✓ Review and determine the current unemployment rate and the long-term employment outlook.

Know the company:

- ✓ Is the company profitable or going through difficult financial times?
- ✓ What is its position in the business cycle (startup, developing, constant, turnaround)?

Know where you stand:

- ✓ Your technical capabilities, expertise and unique selling features.
- ✓ Your resources, including networking contacts.
- ✓ The caliber of your competition and the availability of other candidates in the market.

Know the hiring manager:

- ✓ Is this an urgent position that the company needs to fill?
- ✓ Understand the entire decision-making process, influencers and hiring budget.
- ✓ Is the manager you are interviewing with able to extend an offer, or do they need to go higher up?

Negotiation is an important part of the communication process. It's composed of research and strategy.

In the research stage, gather as much information as you can about your skills, and the company's values and needs. In the strategy stage, use your enthusiasm as a major negotiating technique. When you show energy and a positive attitude, it's hard for any employer to be disinterested in you.

What are your salary requirements?

Once an employer has determined that a candidate is the right fit for the company, the next step is determining the financial feasibility for both parties. Interviewers might ask how much money the candidate makes in their current position. This is a straightforward question and should be answered without hesitation.

Tip: It's best to let the employer know that you will consider the entire compensation package, including benefits, healthcare, 401K, and tuition reimbursement. Also, make sure that the employer is aware you will consider cost of living indexes (if relocation is involved), commuting time, and other factors such as quality of life.

How Do You Handle a Salary History Request?

Most job seekers don't know how to respond when an employer requests a salary history to be submitted with a resume. Nobody wants to price themselves out of a job, but by the same token you do not want to give the employer the opportunity to offer you less than the going rate for the position. Your response to a request for a salary history is best handled in your cover letter. The question should be addressed at the end of the letter, after you've highlighted your skills, background, accomplishments, experience and interest in the position.

Do...

- ✓ **Respond to the question positively without giving any specific amount.** "My salary is in the low 40's."
- ✓ **Mention your desired salary.** If you are responding to this question in an application, you can state "competitive" or "open." You can also state that the salary is negotiable depending on the position, or give a $2,000 to $5,000 range. Caution: Give a range only if you know the market value for the position and for someone with similar skills and background.
- ✓ **Know your salary requirements ahead of time.** Know what you hope to make. These numbers shouldn't be mentioned in your response to the salary history question. You should, however, give this

some thought for when you get to the negotiating phase.
- ✓ **Be prepared to respond to a request for previous salaries in an interview.** It can be handled by responding without stating specific amounts.

Don't...

- ✓ **Include your salary history on your resume.** What's important is what you did in your job, rather than what you were paid.
- ✓ **Lie about your previous pay rate.** Employers can easily verify your salary history through reference checks.

34.) Closing Career Tips

Visualizing to Achieve Greatness

The use of mental visualization can be very helpful in preparing for your interview. Many professional athletes use it as a form of mental exercise before a game or a sporting event. Athletes start by putting themselves in a state of relaxation or meditation. Then they visualize each and every step of their role or responsibility. A skier would visualize the way they would jump off the line, see the slope in their mind, survey the terrain, visualize the flawless moves they will make, think confidently about performing to the absolute best of their abilities and visualize winning the race.

This is not much different than someone preparing for an interview or starting a new job search. The power of positive thinking and mental visualization can go a long way if you use it properly. Visualization has been know to heal the body as well. By using visualization, you can rehearse your coming interview, including how you would react in specific situations and conditions.

In preparation for your interview, go through the motions in your mind. Anticipate the questions which may be asked. Visualize yourself as confident and self-assured. Play the part over and over in your mind until you feel you have truly lived it, and you are ready. Visualize your success until it becomes reality, then go out there and get that job!